PROBLEM SOLVING POWER

How to Create & Apply Successful Personal, Career, & Business Problem-Solving Strategies

*"The Thinker," a sculpture by Auguste Rodin
Created in bronze — 1880 to 1900 A.D.*

By

THOMAS B. FRANKLIN

THE OCTAGON PRESS
P.O. Box 36854
Los Angeles, California 90036

Library of Congress Cataloging in Publication Data:

Franklin, Thomas B., 1935-
Problem Solving Power
Includes bibliographical references.
1. Problem solving. 2. Creative thinking. 3. Thought and thinking.
4. Success. 5. Career development. I. title.
BF455.A43   1989   153   Pending
ISBN 0-925053-00-7 Pbk.

First Edition
Published by the Octagon Press
P.O. Box 36854, Los Angeles, California 90036
Printed in the United States of America
10 9 8 7 6 5 4 3 2 1

Most illustrations in this text are from the following collections:

> *MEN—A Pictorial Archive from Nineteenth Century Sources;* Copyright 1978, Dover Publications, 180 Varick St., N.Y.C., NY 10014.

> *WOMEN—A Pictorial Archive from Nineteenth Century Sources;* Copyright 1978, Dover Publications, 180 Varick St., N.Y.C., NY 10014.

> *CHILDREN—A Pictorial Archive from Nineteenth Century Sources;* Copyright 1978, Dover Publications, 180 Varick St., N.Y.C., NY 10014.

PLEASE BE ADVISED: *This book is provided purely as an educational tool and is not intended in any way to be psychological, legal, business or personal counseling. Furthermore the problem-solving instruction given in this book is intended only for career, business and personal goal problem-solving. No claim is made or intended that the techniques taught in this manual apply to physical, emotional, mental, psychological, psychiatric, legal or other problems addressed by licensed professionals.*

PROBLEM SOLVING POWER

—TABLE OF CONTENTS—

— DEDICATION —

The September, 1979, issue of *Success* magazine featured an interview by senior editor Mary Granius of a man who died on June 7, 1979, the day before the story was completed. I felt that the editor's decision to publish the story in *Success* was the best of all possible ways to honor a man who had faced and solved some of the most difficult of problems on the way to his success.

I have chosen to dedicate my book to him, not because he stands out as the greatest problem-solver of the age, nor even because he exemplifies the struggle of a minority entrepreneur achieving success despite awesome odds against him. No, I have chosen to make this dedication because of *how* he achieved this success and solved his problems. He did the one thing which is prized above all by authors of books such as this one. First he read a book which presented a formula for breaking out of his unwanted, fixed state of existence (in other words, his major, overall problem situation), a step-by-step procedure for reaching the seemingly unattainable objective he envisioned. Not only did he read the book, but he read it over and over until he *understood* it, and then he did something not one in ten thousand ever do: he followed that step-by-step procedure all the way to the achievement of his objective, and even far beyond that achievement!

If this wasn't enough to satisfy the author of a "How to" book on living, this man went even further. He sought out the author and told him of his success, and at the author's insistence, he began to lecture on the procedure and taught the course to about 850 individuals during a seven year period. When he died he still had in his office a loving cup trophy presented to him by the author of the book for having the best success school in the country one year. One of his students was featured in *Black Enterprise* magazine for beginning a $2-million-dollar-a-year hair and beauty aids distribution company out of the trunk of his car.

It has been said that imitation is the greatest of compliments. My dedication of this book to James H. Browne is in recognition of this unique quality he possessed: to totally learn from and apply the writings of a well-written guide to more effective living.

His Story

On September 27, 1945, a railway mail clerk named James H. Browne purchased a self-help book at Caruso's Bookstore in Kansas City, Kansas. Browne hid his book in a paper bag to avoid ridicule from his fellow clerks. In a world where it is commonplace for people to buy books on exercise rather than exercise, and books on dieting rather than control their eating habits, Browne probably realized that it would be assumed that he too was only indulging his fantasies by reading a book on how to get rich. In the end they would expect him to spend the rest of his working life in the civil service just as they would, secure but never rich.

I too have hidden the title of Browne's book from you, because the sheer quantity of how-to-get-rich books on any paperback book display has made every book of this genre seem to be a recipe for wishful thinking. When you see the title of this book, you may share Browne's fellow workers' attitude of ridicule, but I ask you to think again. The first edition of the book Browne read was published in 1937, at a time when the very idea of becoming rich was far more ridiculous than in 1945 or today. More than three million copies of the book have now been sold. Today it is not stylish among business executives to read "outdated" books containing platitudes and "folk wisdom." The only "acceptable" guides to success must be written by Waterman, Peters, Molloy, Drucker or Trump. The idea that there may be timeless, universal principles which apply in any day and age is passed up in favor of technospeak. But James H. Browne demonstrated vividly that well-focused principles, *if followed diligently,* could lead just as surely to success as the fanciest tactics dreamed up by the sharpest strategists in today's marketplace.

After Browne read his how-to-get-rich book, he convinced his fellow mailclerks that he had gone mad by giving up his ten years of seniority with the civil service to become a commission-only insurance salesman. By 1950, James Browne was assistant manager of the Kansas City office of Atlanta Life Insurance Company, and one of it's top producers. He was featured in *Ebony* magazine for selling $161,750 worth of policies in one year (a small amount in today's dollars but a significant accomplishment at that time), and he was honored as one of the top ten black life-insurance salesmen in the United States.

Up to this point Browne had it pretty easy. It was true that his father had died when he was 16 and he had become the sole support of his mother and sister at that early age by working at odd jobs until he graduated from high school (5th in a class of 76 graduates). And it was true that he had sold furniture polish, sung with a quartet, and operated an elevator during the depression until he passed the civil service examination to obtain his job with the post office. Nevertheless, he liked selling insurance and did well at it. He did not start running into serious problems until he decided, along with a close friend and associate, to found and operate *a bank!*

Browne and his associate, H.W. Sewing, immediately encountered skepticism and prejudice on many fronts. There had never been a black-owned-and-operated bank in that part of the midwest. One of the state requirements to become chartered was to obtain a list of persons attesting to the *need* for such a bank to serve the community in question. Efforts to obtain the list of names met with great resistance. Questions were raised about "negro business failures in the community." One black-owned finance company had ended up in receivership and fears were expressed that this venture would end up similarly. Several larger banks in the Kansas City area actively tried to *block* the organizers' attempts to obtain a charter.

One prominent motivational speaker, today in the '80s, likes to say that "90% of failure comes from quitting." This was a principle that Browne and his associate Sewing understood very well. They were determined to convince the Kansas banking board that the black community in Kansas City was not getting adequate banking services, and that their proposed bank would not only fill that need, but would also serve *any* qualified customer. Sewing took off for a three-week tour of eight black-owned banks in the country to gather information and Browne took a crash correspondence course in accounting. As you will see, two fundamentals of problem-solving power were being applied with perfect precision.

Up to this point, H.W. Sewing had been a major source of inspiration for Jim Browne. As manager of the Kansas City office of Atlanta Life Insurance Company, he had given Browne his first sales job. As founder of a short-term installment loan company, Sewing had laid the groundwork for the bank he and Browne would attempt to start. Now it was Browne's turn to become a source of inspiration. He introduced Sewing to two books by the author who had inspired his determination to be a self-made success. Sewing had the perspicacity to realize that one principle in those books could lead to a resolution of their problems and an achievement of their objectives. Together they assembled a "master mind" group which met two or three mornings a week to do what we now call "brainstorming." There they considered how the principles Browne had successfully followed to this point could be applied to fully realize their group objectives.

Gradually the organizers gained the respect and support of the banking community. Eventually one of the largest banks in Missouri even wanted to be their correspondent bank. Their efforts paid off. Douglass State Bank (named for Frederick Douglass, American abolitionist) became a reality. By 1956, Browne had left Atlanta Life Insurance Company, where he had earned his livelihood during the creation of Douglass State Bank, and he opened Crusader Life Insurance Company, which he eventually merged with American Woodmen.

In addition to working as a life insurance salesman and operating the bank, Browne found time to contribute to numerous community projects in Kansas City. One of his numerous awards for service was that of "Outstanding Citizen" presented by the Kansas City Chamber of Commerce. The Chamber sent Browne to represent the U.S. Government at the International Labor Conference in Geneva, Switzerland in 1961. In 1976, he was lauded by President Ford for his work as a member of the national advisory committee to the Small Business Administration, and he was among the top black businessmen invited by President Carter to the White House to provide insight into the condition of black businesses in America.

When Mary Granius interviewed him at the age of 69, in 1979, Browne still had his original copy of Napoleon Hill's *Think and Grow Rich*. He said, "You can see how old this book is now. I have other copies—they were given to me. But I treasure this one because it is the bridge that brought me across. I had never read anything like this before. Other books give you a lot of statistical data and rhetoric. But *Think and Grow Rich* set up, step by step, what you're supposed to do. I've said it over and over again: To me, this book is better than a degree from Oxford. Their degrees are good, but this set it down in such basic principles that, if followed, you could make it."

My Hope

Since Napoleon Hill's *Think and Grow Rich*, literally hundreds of books have been written on the subject, but the vast majority of them are gathering dust on their owner's bookshelves. Perhaps any one of these books could make the owner of it rich if the principles within it were applied with the diligence of a James H. Browne.

It is my grandest hope, as an author, that somewhere a reader as industrious as James H. Browne, will *apply* some of the problem-solving techniques in this book to at least one of the major problems of our society or the world, with the result that even one of those very real problems becomes permanently solved!

Thomas B. Franklin
Los Angeles, California, 1988

There is no confinement more inescapable than the fixed condition into which we often settle when retreating from problems and confusion in life.

– INTRODUCTION –

"If your problem-solving system is so good," I can hear you saying, "who has used it successfully?" The answer to that is *everyone who has ever solved a problem*! This is only true because the system has been built in reverse. It is simply a record of how people have solved problems effectively. The system could be called a "codification" of generally accepted problem-solving principles.

Let me clarify what I mean. If you were here talking with me, I would ask you to name a half-dozen successful people who obviously had to solve a lot of problems on the way up. Since you're not here with me, I'll choose a few people I think you will recognize. Let's start with Colonel Sanders of *Kentucky Fried Chicken* fame, or the founder of *Wendy's Hamburgers* (whose name you wouldn't recognize), or maybe Wally Amos, the founder of *Famous Amos* cookies! How about Carl Karcher, the founder of *Carl's Jr.* restaurants?

I'm sure you'll say, "All of these guys are in the same kind of business. How about some variety?" O.K., I'll bet you've read one of Stephen King's horror stories or you've seen a movie based on one of his books, like *Carrie.* Do you know who made him rich as well as famous? You will soon know! How about Bonnie MacAllister, the first woman ever chosen to be Ohio's "Small Business Person of the Year," who also ranked nationally in the top five "Small Business Persons of the Year." Until she came along no one ever thought of developing a chain of *fingernail care* franchises! Another first was Curt Carlson, the man who started supermarket trading stamps, whose company topped 2 *billion dollars* a few years ago. Now *that* is an interesting story!

I've got one more that should be familiar to those of you on the West Coast. Here in California you can't turn on your TV to watch a late movie without hearing from Cal Worthington ("Go See Cal"), the car man. If you don't see Cal in your part of the country, you're certain to have his counterpart advertising nightly on your TV. Cal sells cars to more than a quarter million people every year. He is the nation's largest car dealer, with dealerships in California, Arizona, and Alaska. By the time you finish this chapter, Cal will have sold four more cars.

The burning question here is: What do all of these guys have in common? Is it possible that every one of them solves problems exactly the same way? To some degree, the answer is "yes," but it would be more accurate to say that they all use the same *basis* for their solutions, although they may not express that basis in the same terms. Initially they might not even agree that there is any similarity in the way they approach problem solving, but upon closer inspection I believe they would recognize the common core concepts. "What makes you so sure?" you are probably asking by now.

One of my goals in writing this book has been to keep the reading fairly easy. Since people who have already solved all of their problems are probably not reading my book, I am addressing it to those of you who have problems and are looking for solutions. The next couple of pages form the basis for the rest of the book. If you can stay with me through this explanation, it will make the rest of the book much more understandable.

Business as a Basis for ALL Human Transactions

People have been in business since the first Neanderthal man traded a dinosaur bone for a necklace of saber-tooth tiger fangs. Whenever it's possible for two human beings to communicate, eventually they will trade something. Business is simply a natural phenomenon. Some people want to plant corn or raise goats or sheep. Others want to hunt or fish and hate planting. It's a sure thing that before very long some trading will go on.

As a child, you may have ventured into business yourself. Perhaps you tried a lemonade stand, sold girl-scout cookies, cut lawns or did baby-sitting. The very minute you started into business, even at the level of a lemonade stand, you created an entire business structure. Let me show you what I mean. You had to have a *production* department to make the lemonade. You had to have the *resources* to make the stand and set it up, and the *financial resources* to have some coins on hand to make change. There had to be some *personnel* to do the work, even if the only person was you. And finally there had to be a *communication and promotion* department to print up a sign that said "Lemonade, two cents a glass."

It's hard to believe, but at the age of five or six you, or one of your friends, may already have had a business concern with *four* departments: (1) production, (2) resources & finance, (3) personnel, and (4) communication & promotion. In fact, actually you probably had a few more departments than that. To make the lemonade, it's likely that you had to get a little help from an older brother or sister or your mother. This would have required some diplomacy and tact, better known in industry as *Public Relations*. This is the department that keeps you on good terms with the community and *contributes* to charities like Public Service TV and Radio, the Cancer Society, and the Heart Foundation.

Besides these "action departments," you needed a department to provide you with the *knowledge* to make the lemonade. In industry, that department would be called "R & D", *Research & Development*.

Another department which was there all along, but is usually i. noticed because it's so close to home, is the *executive* department. You would think of it as "Top Management." This is the prime moving *source* of any business. When *you* decided to put together a lemonade stand, *you* were the top executive, the *creative source* of the entire operation.

Now you have expanded your lemonade stand to *seven* departments without even finishing kindergarten, but there is still a bit more. If that lemonade stand is successful, it is probable you will want to open another lemonade stand down the street, and this means *expansion.* You will need a department of *marketing expansion* to help you grow bigger. Every healthy business owner wants his or her business to grow. It's just a *natural* process. Colonel Sanders and Carl's, Jr. and Wendy's and Cal all followed the same pathway. These departments evolved out of the ways human beings naturally interact. They weren't artificially created. They just developed naturally, and this natural pattern contains some very valuable principles which may help you solve many different kinds of problems.

What Does this Have to Do With Me?

By this time you may have decided that this book isn't for you. If you are not in business and your problems are not business related, it may seem that none of this has anything to do with you. Not so! These eight departments don't apply just to *business* transactions. They apply to *any* interchange between human beings, in personal relationships, in school, at work, within the family, and in social and even international situations. These eight dimensions of life encompass just about everything you do, and everything anyone else does too. Let's see if I can prove my point. First take a look at this diagram of an organization chart. Notice that under each business heading, there is a *personal* equivalent:

Top Management (A Business's Creative Source)
Equivalent: Your Own Creativity

Personnel Mgr.	Advertising & Communication	Financial Mgr.
Your Own Morale	*Your Own Communications*	*Your Own Resources*

Production Manager	Quality Control	Sales & Marketing	Public Relations
Your Time & Productivity Management	*Your Own Knowledge & Skills*	*Your Personal Growth & Expansion*	*Your Contributions & Recognition*

I think now you can see how any problem you might be having would come under one of these departments. Look over this list of problems and see if any of them sound familiar:

★ **Creativity problems:** *Frustration with being unable to come up with creative solutions when you need them.*

★ **Mental, physical, or emotional morale problems:** *Controlling diet, lack of exercise, insufficient rest or recreation, low energy, or self-esteem.*

★ **Communication problems:** *Misunderstandings, upsets, difficulty getting your point across, or getting others to communicate or listen.*

★ **Resource or financial problems:** *Scarcity of needed cash, capital, or other resources.*

★ **Productivity problems:** *Lack of time, failure to finish things, or low energy and achievement.*

★ **Knowledge problems:** *Lack of data or technical expertise or skills. Difficulty studying or completing courses of study.*

★ **Growth and expansion problems:** *Dissatisfaction with job or business. Hard to promote yourself and do better.*

★ **Exchange of help problems:** *A lack of acknowledgment. Difficulty making a contribution or receiving recognition for contributions you do make.*

Do any of your current problems fall into one of these categories?

In the chapters that follow, each of these departments (categories of problems) will be taken up. You'll see how Colonel Sanders and Cal and the boys used this tool, without even realizing it, to break down the problems which came their way, and to thus arrive at appropriate solutions rapidly.

With a little James H. Browne diligence, I believe you'll be able to use this tool, as well as the many other tools you will find in this book, to solve your own problems with an ease you may never have thought possible.

THIS LIFE IS A TEST AND ONLY A TEST.

If it had been
a real life
you would have
been contacted
and told where
to go and what
to do.

*To find a solution, first you must recognize
there is a problem. Next you must face up to
doing whatever you must to solve it.*

1. THE KEY TO INSTANT PROBLEM SOLVING

The first stage in strategic thinking is to
pinpoint the critical issue in the situation.
Kenichi Ohmae: *The Mind of the Strategist*

"*The KEY to instant problem solving.*" It sounds like magic
doesn't it? The penniless, homeless derelict might imagine finding
a shiny key with a bank name and a box number printed on the
side of it. When he goes to that bank, he finds that the key opens
a safety deposit box, containing all of the wealth he needs to solve
every problem he has. Now *that* is a KEY!

Indulge me and follow along through another fantasy. Imagine
you find a key which opens a succession of doors, in a maze, which
eventually leads to a central vault. There, all of the wealth and
knowledge you need to solve your problems is located. At each
point through the maze, however, you are faced with several doors
to choose from, but the KEY will fit only one of them. Without
the key, you would have to break down each of the doors to move
on through the maze, but that would cost you much time and
great effort. With the key, you can simply try it in each door
until you find the one that opens. You can then move on, through
the maze, to the next set of doors. When you arrive there, once
again, the key will open the one door which will lead you, through
the maze, to the prize in the center.

The key I offer you here is more often like the key in the
second fantasy, than the one in the first, although there are times
when just having the key to a single door will reveal the solution
to your problem. The *American Heritage Dictionary* defines
"solution" primarily as: *4. The method or process of solving a
problem,* and *5. The answer to or disposition of a problem.* But
there is another definition of "solution": *7. The action of separating or breaking up; a dissolution,* and *3. The state of being
dissolved.*

To get an idea of this definition of a "solution," picture yourself
traveling along a winding, scenic road, through the mountains or
along the ocean. Suddenly, you come to a turn, and there, in the
middle of the road, is a huge black rock blocking the entire road.
Perhaps this is what a problem feels like to you: a huge, unmovable
obstacle in your way, blocking your path to whatever it is you
would like to be, or do, or obtain in life. If you could simply
dissolve that rock or obstacle in your path, you could move on
to reach your objective. Since the rock is so huge, however, you
may have to "break it up," as suggested by the definition of *solution.*
In this situation, the "key" might be a sledge hammer, a stick of

dynamite or, better yet, a bulldozer. The solution-KEY can be anything which will enable you to break up the obstacle or move it out of your way.

An excellent power tool to start with would be one which, in a single stroke, allowed you to break the obstacle in two. Take a look at our first solving tool, which allows you to do just that.

Separating Growth Problems
from Problems of Decline

In the picture of the rock in the road, we have a classic illustration of a growth-barrier problem. A growth problem is always a problem which stands in the way of forward motion, of greater expansion, or a better life. A problem of decline, on the other hand, is a problem which must be solved to prevent you, or your project, or your company, from sliding backwards or going "down the drain."

It should only take a moment to notice whether a problem you are having is one of growth enhancement, or one of decline prevention. Nevertheless, it is a valuable distinction, to make early on, because your growth problem-solving strategy will be very different from your decline problem-solving strategy. Perhaps the easiest way to determine which category your problem falls into, is to ask yourself: "If I solve this problem, will I be farther along than I have ever been, on the path to reaching my goals in this area, or will I have only corrected errors that have occurred along the way, and regained ground I lost through prior setbacks?"

We can always take on growth problems more easily and enthusiastically than decline problems, because, when we solve a growth problem, we are farther ahead. When we solve a decline problem, we may feel that, at best, we are not as far behind as we were. We're annoyed that we had to stop and solve it at all, but to fail to solve a real problem of decline is to invite further decline and probably eventual disaster. Later in the book, we'll take on the knotty issue of decline problems, but, for now, let's look at the more enjoyable task of solving growth problems.

The Power of Growth Solutions

Many entrepreneurs have achieved fame and fortune by solving the problem of how to make a business grow. R. David Thomas went to work for Colonel Harland Sanders, of *Kentucky Fried Chicken* fame, in 1956. His job was troubleshooting in Sanders' restaurants, which were not yet specializing in fried chicken. In 1958, Thomas convinced Sanders that a restaurant in Ft. Wayne,

Indiana, which featured nothing but chicken, would be successful. Then, in 1962, he accepted an offer from Sanders to go to Columbus, Ohio, to revitalize a faltering chain of six restaurants. Sanders offered him a 40% ownership, *if* he could make them profitable. Thomas changed the menus from over 100 items to just fried chicken, cole slaw, and soft drinks, and he coined the name "Kentucky Fried Chicken." The chain became a solid success. Thomas became a "paper" millionaire and vice president of the company. He had proven to be a master of solving the problems of major growth.

Another Master of Growth Problem Solving

In 1937, Curt Carlson graduated from the Univerity of Minnesota, with a degree in Economics. Job recruiters on campus signed him up as a sales representative, for Proctor & Gamble, selling Oxydol, Camay, Ivory Soap, and Crisco shortening, to small grocers in the Minneapolis area. It was not a glamorous job and, although Carlson became the top salesman in his district in the first six months and eventually one of the two top producers nationally, he was not adequately challenged. While in high school, he often ran three paper routes at one time, worked as a bellhop, and caddied at the local golf course. It seemed he instinctively sought a larger game and bigger problems to solve.

During his first year with Proctor & Gamble, he had a flash of creative inspiration. Einstein once said that creativity is bringing old concepts together in new ways. Trading stamps had existed for forty years, but were only offered by large department stores as merchandise premiums. Carlson got the idea that small grocers could better compete with the big chain stores, if stamps were offered for nationally advertised food items, so he created "Gold Bond" stamps. First he had to convince mom-and-pop grocers, who were steadily losing business to large chains, that they would benefit from paying him what would amount to nearly *two-percent* of their gross! Many would have considered it an impossible task, but Carlson persisted.

Until after the second world war, it was very tough going. Two-thirds of his business was lost when wartime shortages made it unnecessary to stimulate sales with stamp premiums, but, after the war, the chains began to notice the advantage the trading stamps were giving the small independents. A chain called "Super Valu" signed on for the Gold Bond stamps, and, within the first ten months, increased their business by 81 percent!

Carlson's creative idea set a new trend. He sold his plan to many chains across the country, and soon competitive stamp companies entered the market. In 1968, the stamp business totalled $440 billion, and Carlson had a healthy market share. By the 1960s, Carlson realized that the market was over-saturated, so he shifted into hotels, and then into restaurants and, by the 1970s, into ten diverse operating groups. All were part of the Carlson Companies family. In 1974, he gathered together his company presidents and top executives, and announced a goal of *one billion dollars* in business by 1981. The companies reached that goal by 1978. If degrees of excellence were awarded for growth problem-solving mastery, Curt Carlson could be rated a "Supreme Master."

The Stages of Growth

The next "key" to "instant" problem-solving is one that will let you know how far along, through the problem-maze, you have come. With this tool, you will be able to check at any point, to see how you're doing. Have you just *recognized* what the problem is, and started working toward a solution? Or have you just *reviewed* the situation, to see how you got into this problem situation in the first place? Are you now getting *familiar* with the facts and circumstances of the problem and possible solutions? The following *stages of growth* scale, will help you identify exactly how far along you have come, in the problem-solving process.

↑ GROWTH STAGE:

8.   MAXIMIZE
7.   CAPITALIZE
6.   UTILIZE
5.   ORGANIZE
4.   ENERGIZE
3.   FAMILIARIZE
2.   REVIEW/REVISE
1.   RECOGNIZE

There have been many descriptions of the stages of growth, or development, in the individual, in relationships, in careers, in companies, cities, states, and nations. The eight arbitrary stages, which I have chosen to use as a model to evaluate degrees of growth, were inspired by an excellent book on career development, called *Skills for Success,* written in 1979, by Adele M. Scheele, Ph.D. It is based on a series of case studies of successful attorneys and other very successful professionals. Dr. Scheele identified, as a common denominator, six developmental skills, that each of the individuals studied employed to move up the ladder of success. As I studied her six stages of "Career Competencies," it seemed to me that they came close to outlining a universal progression in the stages of growth and development. After viewing the stages of successful development of many business enterprises, over a period of years, I expanded the number of stages to eight, and generalized them into the poetic list presented above, for easy reference.

To make these stages of growth more visual, and easily understood, consider the steps a pilot goes through, in getting an airplane off the ground, and into an ideal long-range flying pattern. First, he must *recognize* and understand the flight plan. He must *review* the suggested flight route, and *revise* it to fit existing weather conditions. He must then *familiarize* himself with the plane he will be flying, and any controls which may be different from those in planes he has flown previously. When everyone is aboard, and all preliminary actions have been completed, he is ready to *energize* the motors and take off. These first four stages are the *launching* steps.

Now the plane is in the air. It is time to *organize* the controls for a long, stable flight. Depending on weather conditions and advance reports from weather stations, located along the flight path ahead, he may adjust his altitude, or mode of flight, to *utilize* tail winds and clear skies to his best advantage. If he is flying in stormy weather, or against fierce head winds, his progress may be slower than usual, and he may find himself running behind schedule. If he suddenly breaks into a patch of clear sky, he may "pour on the power," to *capitalize* on the momentary advantage. If the sky remains clear the rest of the way, he will probably *maximize* his forward motion, in the hope that he will make up the lost time, and possibly even arrive on schedule. He has taken the plane through all of the eight stages, from *recognize*, to *maximize!*

A Natural Progression of Solutions

David Thomas, the originator of the "Kentucky Fried Chicken" concept for Colonel Harland Sanders, *recognized* the need to change the restaurant chain's menu, from the one hundred or more items on it. He saw that it was important to change the *focus* of the restaurant to just a few items with very broad appeal. He *reviewed* sales records of the chain, and *revised* the menu to just fried chicken, cole slaw, and soft drinks, based on his evaluation of that review. At this point, he undoubtedly *familiarized* himself with the competition, and the attitude of the buying public toward this revised image, before he *energized*, and launched his new operation. From that point on, it was simply a question of *organizing* the new operation carefully, and *utilizing* a smaller crew more efficiently. Judging from the rapid success of the *Kentucky Fried Chicken* chain, Thomas must have *capitalized* on every advantage that came his way, until he had *maximized* his own profits to become a "paper millionaire."

Curt Carlson's successes could be followed through these same stages of development, as well. They are simply a way of describing a natural progression.

Checklists as the Key to Solutions

At this moment, you may be at any one of these eight stages, of progress (or decline), in your efforts to solve a problem. Picture yourself in the maze I described earlier. You have reached a juncture where there are a dozen doors to choose from. Your first step, is to identify the correct door to open next. The KEY will fit only one lock perfectly, although you may be able to force it into one of the others. At the end of this chapter you will find a "Checklist Key." At the end of every chapter in this book, there is a related checklist. This "Key List" gives you a quick look at each of those checklists.

Keeping your specific problem in mind, you can look at the summary of each of these checklists. That will allow you to pick out the list which best applies to your present stage of development, in solving your problem. If you prefer, you can read the chapter which precedes that checklist, before you answer the questions or carry out the instructions in it, or you can simply do the checklist. The choice is yours. Used with patience and persistence, these KEYS can unlock the door to a solution for any problem.

You will notice, there are several checklists for the first stages of development. Effective solutions usually require a lot more work early on. It's like taking a trip. If you map out exactly where you're going, *before* starting out, you can save a great deal of aimless driving later. It may take working through several checklists, to really *recognize* the problem, to *review* all of the factors leading up to it, to *revise* your strategy, and to *familiarize* yourself with the components needed to carry it out. Nevertheless, the time will be well spent, because, when you begin to *energize* and *organize* your solution strategy, you are likely to find that part to be an effortless task.

My observations have so completely convinced me that the greatest difficulty in resolving problems lies in the beginning stages, that I have dedicated much of this book to developing the skills you need to accomplish these early steps well. During the years I worked as a career consultant, I found one phenomenon occurring regularly. In a consultation session, I would help a client carefully work out a series of actions, to carry out during the coming week or two. At the beginning of the next session, we would go over the list of actions to see what had been accomplished. Some clients would complete seven out of ten items; others would complete as few as three out of ten. What was initially puzzling, was the fact that one or two particular actions would remain on the list, week after week. While everything else was being accomplished, those items would not even be approached. I quickly learned that:

Any task which is scheduled, and not accomplished, needs to be undercut and broken down into smaller tasks.

This might seem like quite a simple rule, but it can apply over and over again. After breaking an item down into several smaller tasks, I would sometimes find that one or more of those smaller tasks *still was not being accomplished!* That meant reducing those tasks into even *tinier* steps. Or finding out what *resistance* there might be to accomplishing those steps. In Chapter 5, on *Morale Power,* you will find a discussion on purpose, motivation, and pride, which relates directly to this issue.

A Responsibility KEY Checklist

Apparently medical doctors encounter difficulty in treating patients as frequently as I did in counseling job-seekers. Dr. Bernard Siegel, M.D., author of *Love, Medicine and Miracles* (Harper & Row), has developed four vital questions to determine whether patients will respond favorably to medical treatment. He asks:

1. Do you want to live to be 100? *(This indicates whether the person feels in control of life and looks forward to the future.)*
2. What does your current disease mean to you? *(This indicates whether the illness is seen as a challenge to be overcome, or as an overwhelming obstacle.)*
3. Why do you need this illness? *(To some degree this can indicate whether or not the illness is serving some psychological purpose.)*
4. What happened in the year or two before you got sick? *(90% of cancer patients interviewed had experienced a significant change in their lives during the previous two years.)*

Dr. Siegel reports that only 15 to 20% of the people interviewed were ready to approach their illness with a thrust toward survival! He also says that, only when a patient indicates a willingness to take responsibility for his or her illness and to participate in the recovery, can that recovery occur.

A similar series of questions could be posed to any individual with a problem:

1. Are you looking forward to the time when your problem is solved?
2. Are you viewing your problem as a challenge or as an insurmountable obstacle?
3. Is your problem *needed* to serve any psychological or emotional purpose?
4. What events led up to this problem which could account for your having it?

Just as Dr. Siegel notes that an individual must be willing to take responsibility for a disorder, and to participate in his or her own recovery before it can take place, so the person with a problem must be willing to take responsibility for that problem, and *actively seek* a solution in order to find one.

A KEY to Unlock Three Main Doors

The next chapter will introduce you to some common problem-solving sequences. The first three stages of nearly every approach to solving are to:

(1)   Define the problem,
(2)   Gather information, and
(3)   List all solution options.

It has been my experience in doing problem-solving consulting, that when an applied solution fails, it is because (1) the problem wasn't adequately defined, (2) not enough information was collected or checked for accuracy, or (3) not enough options were considered before settling on a solution to implement. The first KEY, therefore, is actually a trio, consisting of *definition, knowledge,* and *scope.* You will find that 80%, or more, of every chapter, will be spent on getting you to: (1) define the problem from different points of view, (2) focus on gathering facts and resources, and (3) consider a *very* wide range of options.

There are two old proverbs which some have said contradict each other: "Look before you leap," and "He who hesitates is lost." I believe that both of these are true, if you follow the sequence correctly. The KEY to instant problem-solving is to LOOK thoroughly before you take action. When you are *certain* that you have done your best to look at all of the factors, then *don't hesitate* to take action. After all, the final stage of problem-solving is to get feedback on what happened when you applied your solution; then to *review and revise* it, if it didn't work, and go through the process again and again until you get the result you desire.

PROBLEM SOLVING POWER
CHECKLIST ONE: KEYLIST

ONE (Key List): Select appropriate list.

TWO (Recognize): Is there really a problem? Do you really want to solve it? Are you willing to do whatever it takes to solve it? *(If unsure, go to Checklist Two)*

THREE (Review): What is your problem? How does this problem compare to previous problems? Separate this problem from other problems you have.
(If you need help, do Checklist Three)

FOUR (Review): Define your problem by stating: What objective is this problem preventing you from reaching? What obstacles are in your way? *(Have you defined your problem fully? If not, do Checklist Four now)*

FIVE (Revise): How strongly are you motivated to solve your problem? Check your enthusiasm, morale and determination to follow through to arrive at a solution.
(To increase motivation, go to Checklist Five)

SIX (Familiarize): Separate the facts from assumptions, conjecture and other arbitraries. *(Is there still uncertainty or confusion? Do Checklist Six to get focused)*

SEVEN (Familiarize): Examine your intuitive feelings about the problem, people involved in the problem and possible solutions. What would happen if you were willing to "just know" the best way to solve the problem? *(To assist your intuitive powers, go to Checklist Seven)*

EIGHT (Energize): What lack of communication is keeping your problem persisting? What communication might quickly lead to a solution? *(To focus on effective communications, go to Checklist Eight)*

NINE (Organize): What creative idea or innovation, if applied, could rapidly resolve your problem situation? *(To jog your creativity, go to Checklist Nine)*

TEN (Utilize): If you could obtain any resource you wanted, what resource would guarantee a resolution of your problem? Who could supply you with that resource if they chose to? *(To optimize resource use, go to Checklist Ten)*

ELEVEN (Utilize): What problem are you not having? What are you not doing to solve your problem? What approach to solving your problem have you not yet considered? *(To use the full "Power of the Negative" go to Checklist Eleven)*

TWELVE (Capitalize): Who could most thoroughly help you solve your problem? What help could you offer in exchange? *(To master the rules of effective asking, go to Checklist Twelve)*

THIRTEEN (Maximize): How has your problem interrupted your forward progress? When did it happen? Why? How might you get things moving again? *(To maximize your forward progress, go to Checklist Thirteen)*

MASTER CHECKLIST: Viewed on a scale from zero (completely stopped) to ten (completely resolved), where are you now in your progress toward solving your problem? Identify the exact steps necessary to move up from step to step until you reach an ideal solution for your problem.

*Often we must take risks to reach out and
discover new ways to solve problems.*

*By vigorously exercising your problem-solving ability
you can greatly strengthen your mental sharpness.*

2. WHY PROBLEMS DON'T GET SOLVED

"Too many people spend time finding the answer— far too few spend time finding out what the problem is."
—Peter Drucker

People have been devising problem solving methods since the first cave man realized that he had a problem. Ancient scriptures contained methods for solving specific kinds of problems, with the advice being attributed to a God or Gods. The Greeks gave us an entirely new look at solving the problems of life through the words of Aristotle, Socrates, and Plato. From this cradle of new thinking, writers of poetic, moral and practical advice sprang forth in great numbers: Sophocles, Euripides, Herodotus, Aristophanes, Demosthenes, Mencius, Publilius Syrus, Seneca, Plutarch, Marcus Aurelius, just to name a few. What is most fascinating in reading the words of these ancient advisors is how applicable their suggestions often are to the problems of today. It doesn't seem that human nature or human problems have changed that much in two thousand years.

In a case of dissension, never dare to judge 'til you've heard the other side.
Euripides—485-406 B.C.

Practice yourself . . . in little things, and thence proceed to greater.
Epictetus—A.D. 50-120

Search men's governing principles and consider the wise, what they shun and what they cleave to.
Marcus Aurelius Antoninus—A.D. 121-180

Problem solving approaches, however, have changed greatly over the years. The magazine *The Nation's Business* put out a series of articles on problem solving and management decision making in the 1970s. One article focused on a problem-solving program developed by the U.S. Air Force and required in the curriculum of the Air University at Maxwell Air Force Base near Montgomery, Alabama. The approach used involves six steps:

1. Identify the problem.
2. Gather data.
3. List possible solutions.

4. Test possible solutions.
5. Select the best solution.
6. Put the solution into action.

Approximately these same steps were presented in a recent workshop with the following modifications:

1. Recognize, accept the problem & be willing to solve it.
2. Understand, analyze and define the problem. Set goals.
3. Research all pertinent information to reaching a solution.
4. List all alternative solutions & ways to reach goals.
5. Select the best solution, trying the most logical solutions first.
6. Put the solution into action.
7. Evaluate the effect or results of the action taken.
8. Repeat as necessary.

A graphic model of a computerized problem-solving process might look like this:

(INPUT)—(VERIFY)—(PROGRAM)—(TEST)—(OUTPUT)—(REVIEW)

These problem-solving phases also relate to the *stages of growth* itemized in the previous chapter, but they also suggest a *down side* with corresponding *stages of decline.*

The Stages of Growth and Related Problems

GROWTH STAGE:	Potential Problem:
8. MAXIMIZE	Tend to culminate
7. CAPITALIZE	Tend to dissipate
6. UTILIZE	Tend to stagnate
5. ORGANIZE	Tend to disintegrate
4. ENERGIZE	Tend to separate
3. FAMILIARIZE	Tend to terminate
2. REVIEW/REVISE	Tend to spectate
1. RECOGNIZE	Tend to fabricate

It has been said, "If you're not part of the solution, you're part of the problem." How a person handles each of these stages of growth (or decline) may determine where he or she falls on an imaginary scale between "super-solver" and "super-problem" (see *Solver Evaluation Chart.*)

Here is a graphic look at how the growth stages would align

SOLVER EVALUATION CHART

Copyright 1988, Thomas B. Franklin — OCTAGON PRESS, Box 36854, Los Angeles, CA 90036

PERSONAL DEPARTMENT ↓	SUPER SOLVER	SOLVER JR.	SEMI-SOLVER	PROBLEM MAKER	SUPER PROBLEM
MORALE & CONFIDENCE	Leaps tall buildings in a single bound	Takes running start to leap buildings	Leaps only short buildings	Crashes into buildings	Cannot recognize buildings
KNOWLEDGE & INTELLIGENCE	Can read doctor's prescription	Understands IRS tax forms	Can always refold road map	Confuses gas pump hose & water hose	Collapses going up down escalator
CREATIVITY POWER	Walks on water	Swims in water	Washes with water	Drinks the wash water	Passes water in an emergency
RESOURCES & STRENGTH	Stronger than a locomotive	Stronger than a bull elephant	Strong as a bull	Shoots the bull	Smells like a bull
SPACE & TIME EXPANSION POWER	Accurately predicts future events	Anticipates future events	Guesses about the future	Doesn't know what is happening now	Where the hell am I?
PRODUCTIVITY SPEED POWER	Faster than a speeding bullet	Fast as a speeding bullet	Would you believe a slow bullet?	Unable to cock his gun	Shoots self in the foot
COMMUNICATION POWER	Talks directly to "The Force"	Talks with extra-terrestrial beings	Talks to himself	Argues with himself	Loses arguments with himself
HELPING POWER	Carries old ladies over busy street	Helps scout escort lady across street	Can cross at light without help	Needs hand to hold to cross street	Thinks green light is X-mas ornament

with the stages of problem-solving:

INPUT	VERIFY	DESIGN	TEST	OUTPUT
Recognize	Review	Revise	Familiarize	Energize
Recognize	Review	Revise	Familiarize	Organize
Recognize	Review	Revise	Familiarize	Utilize
Recognize	Review	Revise	Familiarize	Capitalize
Recognize	Review	Revise	Familiarize	Maximize

After each pass through the problem solving process, you come back to the beginning of the *Stages of Growth* and go up that ladder another notch. The process is similar to "looping back" in a computer program.

Tendencies Which Prevent Solutions

You can see from these diagrams, that working through the problem-solving process will take you all the way up through the *Stages of Growth*, but there are powerful traps waiting for you as you attempt to climb that ladder. At each point along the way, there appears to be a strong inclination to DECLINE rather than GROW. You might also think of this as a SUCCESS/FAILURE SPECTRUM. At each step up the ladder toward a successful solution, there is an equal possibility of failure at that step. You may have experienced these negative tendencies yourself, as you struggled to solve one problem or another. Take a look at them. See if they seem familiar:

Recognize, Don't Fabricate!

At the beginning point where you sought to *recognize* exactly what the problem was, and to recognize what you should do about it, you may have felt a strong temptation to *fabricate* (or imagine) an easy way out. The race tracks and gambling casinos are crowded with people who are seeking to solve their financial problems with that illusory "lucky break." I'm certain you've been hit up for a "loan" at one time or another by a down-and-out friend who continually fabricated stories of "that big break that was just around the corner."

People whose mind is *fixed* on a fabricated illusion have great difficulty *recognizing* the reality of their true problem situation. As a result, their efforts are never focused in a direction that will enable them to solve their basic problems or break out of an undesirable mode of living. I was originally educated in music and taught and performed music during my early working years. One of my jobs was accompanying musicians and singers in a recording studio. There seemed to be an endless stream of would-be stars who risked

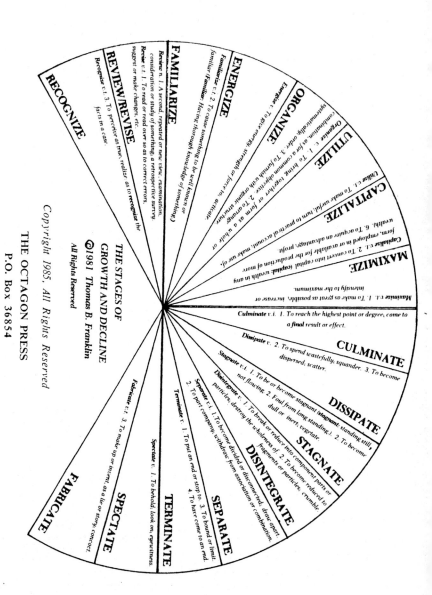

THE STAGES OF
GROWTH AND DECLINE

©1981 Thomas B. Franklin

All Rights Reserved

Copyright 1985, All Rights Reserved

THE OCTAGON PRESS
P.O. Box 36854
Los Angeles, California 90036

all of their extra money making demo records to take around to the studios. Although most of them never achieved any success in music, some at least *enjoyed the process.* As you might suppose, there were others who were fanatical in their lust for stardom, some to the point of absurdity. One such individual was a fellow who had grown up down the street from Elvis Presley and knew Elvis when he was a truck driver. He always said, "if a jerk like Elvis could make it, I can't miss!" The trouble was that this fellow had no sense of timing and his original songs were atrocious. He spent all of the energy and vitality of his youth pursuing his fabricated illusion, and soon found himself overwhelmed with financial problems with no propect of repaying his debts. He was unable to *recognize* the reality of his situation.

To be an effective problem solver you must have the *courage to recognize* the reality of your problem situation and to resist *fabricating* fantasies which will only prolong the problem. Winston Churchill said "Facts are better than dreams." In the chapter which focuses on *Knowledge Power,* you will find some guidelines on separating facts from false assumptions and conjectures.

Have you *recognized* exactly what your problem is and what you may have to do to solve it? If not, this may be the place for you to start.

Review and Revise, Don't Just Spectate!

The next step after *recognizing* the reality of a problem situation, is to *review* the circumstances leading up to that situation, with an eye to *revising* that aspect of your life which brought about the problem. If you have had a problem of any magnitude for a period of time, a sort of *inertia* can set in and it becomes more and more difficult to get into action and do something about it. There is a tendency to fall into *spectatorism,* that is, just sitting back and watching the days go by while the problem gets worse and worse.

In my capacity as a career consultant, I counseled some of the auto workers who were laid off when a major General Motors plant closed. There were two responses to the problem of sudden unemployment. Those who were alert and motivated to handle the situation realized that they might have to look in new directions. They were willing to *review* their job skills and *revise* those skills by seeking job re-training. Others sat back on their unemployment benefits and let opportunities slip by. They chose to be spectators "while Rome burned." I saw a similar phenomenon in the typesetting industry. For many years typesetting was done by casting letters in hot lead. Men who worked in the industry were apprenticed and became journeymen. They had a strong union and job security. Then computers began to change their industry altogether. For the first time women began owning typesetting companies because they were fast typists and could operate the new computerized systems. Soon the union became weak and even the pension fund went broke. Meanwhile many of old "hot metal typesetters" refused to *review and revise* their situation. They too *spectated* "while Rome burned."

To move up and out of an unwanted, fixed set of circumstances, you must have the determination to *trace back* to the point where things first got off course, and then to *plot a corrected course* which will lead to a desirable end result. In the chapter on *Production Flow*, you will find a procedure for locating obstructions in your forward movement and a strategy for getting back on course.

Part of the process of tracing back to find out where things got off course, involves finding any incorrect information, false "facts," bad advice and outright deception. This is the *verify* step in the process. It's never pleasant to contemplate the possibility that you have been misinformed, misled or just plain duped! I have known a number of people who have fallen for financial scams and lost many thousands of dollars. Only by recognizing when, where and why they accepted false information could they then *revise* their approach to investing and save themselves from falling into the trap of another scam. To discover that you have been naive, imperceptive or just plain stupid is a real blow to your morale—your pride and sense of self-respect. In the chapter on *Morale Power*, you will find a series of steps for setting priorities and rebuilding confidence and self-respect.

The KEY to keeping out of the trap of falling into *spectatorism* is to drive with one eye on the rear-view mirror. When you're working on a long-term problem, make a "road map" showing (1) when and where you started, (2) exactly what your ideal destination will be, (3) what route you have taken along the way, and (4) where you are *now* in terms of progress toward your ultimate destination. Update your map regularly so you always *know where you are!*

Have you reviewed the road that led to whatever problem situation you are facing today? Take advantage of this opportunity right now, to find out where you've come from, where you are and where you're going!

Familiarize, Don't Terminate!

It has been said that 90% of failure is the result of *quitting!* Those who persist may eventually succeed. Those who don't persist have no chance of success. As a career counselor, I often talked to people who had *recognized* the need to change jobs. They had *reviewed* their experience and skills and decided to *revise* their workplace or even their occupations. Up to this point the whole thing was mainly a mental exercise, but now it was time to go out and make *real contact* with prospective employers. After two or three rejections, many job-seekers retreated to the security of their existing jobs, only to curse themselves after another two or three stultifying, stagnating years.

The *familiarizing* process can be stressful and even painful. One must put on his or her best face and be judged in the marketplace over and over again. This is not just true of job-seekers. Sales people face this process day after day. The individual starting in a new school, a new job, a new love relationship or just living in a new neighborhood must struggle with the task of grasping new surroundings. Often it means mastering new skills and adjusting to new people's habits, likes and dislikes. It can be a very demanding experience. Many people just choose to *terminate* the entire process, to quit, to give up and return to the old, undesirable yet familiar circumstances.

To be an effective problem-solver you must be able to "stand the heat" of asking, presenting, enduring refusals and asking or presenting again and again. You can take heart from the assurance of the poet Robert Frost, who said, "The best way out is always *through.*" If you press on and go *through* the feelings of fear and doubt and perhaps even despair without giving up, the exhilaration of achievement on the other side will be *proportional* to the degree of difficulty you have encountered.

The *familiarizing* step is also the stage of problem-solving where you begin to *design* a tentative solution to the problem. This is the step where the facts and ideas and opinions which have been collected begin to come together and point toward a creative solution. In the next chapter, you will find many new ways to define your problem. Each of these will open a new possible approach to designing a solution. Then, in the chapter on *Creativity Power*, you will be asked to *create* solutions. These may help you break out of fixed patterns of thinking and direct you toward innovative solving approaches. They can put you further along the way to becoming a "super solver."

When you're struggling to solve a problem and you begin to feel it's futile—no solution is in sight and you feel like giving up—*familiarize* is the KEY which unlocks the next door in the maze. When you begin to feel overwhelmed, the rule is: *Don't quit; LOOK some more!*

Have you taken the time to really examine the people, places, and events surrounding your problem situation? If not, there is a good chance that may be the reason you still have the problem.

Energize, Don't Separate!

The *energizing* zone is the most dangerous zone of all. Most airplane crashes occur either during take-off or during landing. Most new business enterprises fail in the first year or two. Many marriages fall apart before the first year is over. In the U.S., we have seen our space agency lose millions of dollars and destroy the lives of several of our best astronauts in a failed launch effort. Similarly you may have found that, in the process of attempting to solve a very big problem, you have done your homework, you have gathered all of the data you could find and you formulated a "sure-fire plan." Then it was time to *energize* and launch your applied solution. Suddenly your best laid plan wasn't working! Murphy's Law was working overtime! Everything was going wrong. What was going on?

There can be great danger in treating a launching situation as "just another casual experience," whether its a new job, marriage, business or space shuttle. It can be a very great error to go along and conduct "business as usual." An experienced pilot knows that it takes an *enormous thrust* to get that large piece of metal we call an airplane up off of the ground, through the pull of gravity, and up into a level flight path where he can cruise safely for hours. Experienced entrepreneurs know that most businesses lose money the first year and possibly even two years. They are prepared to go the distance. They have set aside their reserves before even beginning. Those who fail usually do so out of an *unrealistic sense of optimism*. They are *energizing* when they have not yet *recognized* what the problems are and what they must do. They are still back there, *fabricating* an imagined business success which cannot occur unless they really work through the intervening steps and stages.

I'm sure you can imagine that these same rules apply equally to beginning a new marriage or personal relationship, but I leave it to you to work out such a delicate enterprise.

Dr. Adele Scheele in her book, *Skills for Success*, describes this stage of development as "Risking-Linking." Think about the concept of "energizing" for a moment. When you energize your radio or TV or toaster, you *plug it in* to a wall socket. You *connect* with the electrical current which is the source of the power that energizes these appliances. In your automobile your fuel line and spark plugs make possible the series of small explosions which energize the motor of your car. Without the linking or connecting of all of these components, there would be no motion. Your car would be a very large, metallic decoration in your driveway. People also speak of making "connections" to progress in business, and politicians exist almost exclusively as a result of their many individual and group contacts.

Very often the *quality of your connections* will determine the successful outcome of a problem resolution or new enterprise. I have traced back times in my life when I failed to resolve a crisis or got into a problem situation that I couldn't easily resolve. I found that in every instance I had (1) *connected* foolishly to people who were either criminals or parasites or simply unreliable in following through on their commitments, or (2) I had foolishly *disconnected* from people who played vital, reliable supporting roles in whatever project I was pursuing at the time.

Over the years, whenever I made my success dependent on unethical or unreliable individuals, failure was almost guaranteed. There was a KEY solving concept that I had not yet realized fully:

> *To energize any effective action, you must connect to reliable power sources, and remain connected without separating until that project or activity is off the ground.*

Imagine cutting the fuel line in a plane while it's in the air, or pulling the plug on a power knife or saw when you're making a vital cut!

On a personal level, your *most* reliable power source is your own education, training, knowledge and experience, but no one can know everything. Eventually we all must rely on others for special skills and abilities. At such times it is *vital* to correctly evaluate who will be a power connection and who will be a power drain. Have you determined who or what is the source of power to best energize the solution to your problem? If not, that may be your next vital step.

Organize, Don't Disintegrate!

By the time you've carried a solution or a project through the *energize* state, and perhaps recycled back through review, revise, and familiarize a few times, chances are you are beginning to get things under control. You have made it through the *critical zone*. Now it's just a matter of getting organized, utilizing your resources effectively, capitalizing on opportunities which come your way, and persisting until you've gotten the maximum value from your efforts.

Nevertheless, there are still some hazards along the way. Very few people are really fond of *organizing* things, and yet the failure to do so will eventually result in things falling apart *(disintegrating)*. Have you taken the time to carefully *organize* a solving strategy? If you are ready to do so, the ideas in the chapter on *Creativity Power* (Chapter 9), and the chapter on *Productivity Power* (Chapter 13), may be what you need next.

Utilize, Don't Stagnate!

Stagnating, the next trap you will probably encounter, is a condition which I have found disturbing to people in all professions. It seems Man in general has a natural inner desire to grow, to improve, to continually have better living standards and a better environment. I have found that blue collar workers, white collar workers and executives all said the same thing when they felt *underutilized* on their jobs: they felt they were *stagnating* at what they were doing. If they continued, they felt they would indeed begin to fall apart (disintegrate, separate, terminate). Look at these definitions of "stagnant": *Foul from standing still; polluted; stale.* Also: *Lacking liveliness or briskness; inactive; sluggish.* Vivid descriptions, I'm sure you'll agree. Little wonder that people eagerly look to escape a *stagnant* position!

The time to take action is when you first notice you are stagnating. The KEY to solving this problem is to shift from the *decline* side of the spectrum to the *growth* side. You can start most effectively by increasing the *utilization* of more and more of your knowledge, skills, talents and total resources. Chapter Ten on *Resource Power* should help you stretch your awareness of the many resources you have at your disposal, when you've made up your mind to go forward. On the decline side, problems *will* begin to multiply. On the growth side, positive momentum can be gained as one problem after another yields to the "liveliness and briskness" of a SOLVER in fast forward motion!

Do you feel you are *utilizing* all of your capabilities and resources as you attempt to solve the problems of life which face you? If not, your next best step may be to work through Chapter 10, *Resource Power.*

Capitalize, Don't Dissipate!

Dissipating (scattering or *wasting)* opportunities and momentary advantages almost guarantees getting stuck at one fixed level and eventually *stagnating.* The KEY to *capitalizing* is staying alert to the probability that opportunities will come by, and being ready to take instant action when they do. Max Gunther, in his indispensable book, *The Luck Factor,* says:

> *". . . little bits of potential luck drift past nearly everybody
> from time to time. But they are only of value to those bold
> enough to reach out and grasp them."*

In Chapter Five you'll find the story of Cal Worthington, the nation's largest car dealer. Cal likes to speak to groups of young people on the subject of success. He tells them that success is largely a matter of spotting the lucky opportunities which come along and acting on them. He says, "Many of us get stuck in the wrong jobs. I see truck drivers who could be great politicians and clerks who should be doctors. We're just not realizing our tremendous potential." He achieved success by *recognizing* doors of opportunity when they opened up for him, and by *capitalizing* on those opportunities.

Are there opportunities open to you which you have not *capitalized* on, in your efforts to resolve your problem? Have you let some chances to resolve your problem slip through your fingers? If so, it may be useful for you to check out Chapter 11, *The Power of the Negative.* You may especially benefit from doing the checklist for that chapter.

You need to keep alert to *seize* every opportunity that arises which offers a possible solution to one of your elusive, long-term problems. Eventually a window of opportunity will open up, if only for a brief moment. The KEY is to *capitalize* on it when it does!

Maximize, Don't Culminate!

Culminating means reaching a conclusion: "The End!" In fairy tales the prince wins the princess and they "live happily ever after." In real life the prince may solve the problem of how to win the princess, but after he wins her he then must solve all of the problems of how to "live happily ever after." *Maximize* is the top of the ladder of the Stages of Growth. *Culminate* begins the fall down the *decline* side because:

EVERYTHING ALIVE IS EITHER GROWING
OR DYING—NOTHING STAYS THE SAME.

Cardinal Newman said it well: "Growth is the only evidence of life." When you stop growing, you begin to decline. Carl Jung, the famous psychologist, said that you should live your life as though you would live forever. People abandon dreams and goals because they think, "I am too old," or "it's too late." Jung advised learning new skills and taking up new pursuits regardless of age. Pablo Picasso was still painting at the age of 91, and Grandma Moses at 101. Verdi composed "Falstaff" at 80, Arturo Toscanini performed until he was 87, and Artur Rubinstein still performed in his nineties. When problems of a lack of vitality or purpose set in, the KEY is to continue to look for a way to grow and to share, regardless of how successful you have become.

Have you reached a point where no further growth seems possible? It is unlikely, but if so, go immediately to Chapter 14, *Expansion Power*. Do the checklist to that chapter very carefully. You may find a means of revitalizing your whole life!

Why Problems Don't Get Solved

Many problems go unsolved because people give up. If some problem is standing in the way of your enjoying life to the fullest, it's not too late to solve it. The very decision to do something about it will fill you with new vigor and life and determination.

You may even have to start at the bottom of the growth scale again. Apparently the scale repeats. Like the fairy tale of the prince and the princess, when you have *maximized* the solving of one set of problems, you may very well find that you will now *recognize* a new set of problems on a higher level to work on. The KEY to solving them is to *welcome the challenge!*

Man's problem-solving skill is the equivalent of the tiger's claws, the antelope's speed, the bull's strength. It is Man's primary survival characteristic. Every problem solved strengthens that ability in the individual, and thereby strengthens his or her potential for longer, more abundant survival.

PROBLEM SOLVING POWER
CHECKLIST   NUMBER   TWO

1 - (Recognize) Is there really is a problem?

2 - If there really is a problem, is it *your* problem or someone else's? Who is really responsible?

3 - Have you *recognized* what it might take to solve this problem? Or have you imagined that it might resolve by itself?

4 - Have you considered what actions of yours have brought about this problem situation and begun to look for ways to revise and resolve it? Or are you simply *spectating* while the problem continues on?

5 - Do you really *want* to solve the problem? Are you willing to do whatever it takes to solve it? Or have you decided to give up because it may be too much for you to take on?

6 - Are you willing to form a well-organized plan to resolve your problem? Or have you allowed the situation to *disintegrate* to the point where a solution seems impossible?

7 - Are you willing to connect to people, places, knowledge and inspiration to resolve your problem? Or have you isolated and *separated* yourself from anyone or anything that might help you find a solution?

8 - Do you agree that a problem usually *can* be solved and that you have the power to bring together the elements needed to solve it? Or are you allowing yourself to remain stuck in your problem situation and *stagnate* there?

9 - Are you ready to watch carefully for opportunities on which you might *capitalize* to resolve your problem? Or do you have a tendency to waste them and let them slip by?

10 - Have you accepted the need to continue moving forward so you can *maximize* your potential? Or have you allowed yourself to reach a peak position and culminated rather than seeking to resolve barriers to further growth?

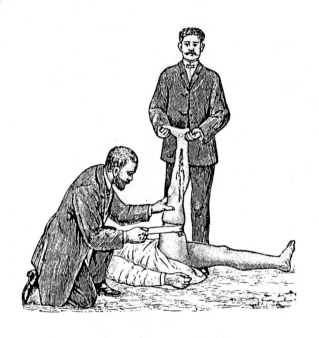

Applying a bandaid will usually not solve a problem; the underlying cause must be discovered and corrected.

When you know what you wish to accomplish and which way to proceed, you will go forward more confidently.

3. YOU CAN'T SOLVE IT IF YOU DON'T KNOW WHAT IT IS!

Define: 1. Determine, entitle, label, designate, characterize, elucidate, interpret, illustrate, represent, individuate, find out, popularize, spell out, translate, exemplify, specify, prescribe. 2. Set limits, bound, confine, limit, outline, fix, settle, circumscribe, mark boundaries, separate out, curb, edge, border, enclose, rim, encircle, envelop.

—Webster's New World Thesaurus

Before you can solve a problem, you must first define it. You can see from the list of synonyms given in Webster's *Thesaurus* that there are many ways to "define" anything. When it's a problem that you're going to define, there are special benefits to be derived from defining it in as many ways as you can. The first fundamental rule of solving problems is:

THE MORE VIEWS OF A PROBLEM YOU CAN GET, THE BETTER YOUR CHANCES OF SOLVING IT.

Before we begin to look specifically at ways to solve problems, let's look at some definitions until we find one that you feel really enables you to define *your* problem!

The *American Heritage Dictionary* starts out by defining a problem as: *"A question or situation that presents uncertainty, perplexity or difficulty."* To give additional depth to that definition, we can take the word "perplexity" and look at its meaning more closely. To "perplex" means *"To confuse or puzzle; to bewilder."* From this we can assume that if you are confused, puzzled, bewildered, and in a difficult or uncertain situation, then you have a problem. Does this sound like it describes you and your problem? If not, let's look further.

The *American Heritage Dictionary* also defines a problem (definition number two) as "A person who is difficult to deal with." Can a person be a problem? I'll let you be the judge of that. If your problem *is* a person, the solution you seek may be much harder to find than a solution for any other kind of problem! But it is also true that if your problem *is* a person, the more thoroughly you "define" the problem the greater the possibility that you will find a satisfactory way to handle that problem person.

The list of synonyms for "define," noted above from the Thesaurus, should give you some idea of how many viewpoints you could have on one single problem. If this is beginning to sound like a riddle, don't be surprised. In a way, that's what problems are all about.

When the Problem Mainly Exists in Your Inner World

Many problems you encounter may be better defined by the definition of a psychological problem: "*A conflict of thoughts, emotions or other forces which results in a full or partial paralysis of constructive action.*"

A while back a lady came to me for a problem-solving consultation relating to her career. She had retired from teaching school and wanted to get back into the work force in a new and interesting occupation. She had tried a number of jobs but none seemed to satisfy her need for an inspiring challenge. After a while, she began to despair of ever finding such a job. She stopped trying and settled into what felt more and more to her like a meaningless existence. When she came to me I put her through the usual career development and aptitude tests to see if I could help her find a direction that felt right to her.

We worked together for several sessions but nothing seemed to inspire her. Gradually, however, I began to notice several factors which fit the "*paralysis of constructive action*" definition. She had an inheritance due her which was tied up in the courts because one relative was contesting some aspect of the will. At first she had attempted to straighten out the problem but found the effort emotionally draining, so she decided to leave the problem to the lawyers.

Another aspect of her life which was in a state of "paralysis" was her relationship with her son. He was in Hawaii, and after many years of close communication with her, he had suddenly stopped writing or calling for nearly a year. She learned from calling his friends that he was well and working, but he seemed to have completely withdrawn from her. Regardless of what activity she became involved in, she was never completely free from worrying about why he had cut himself off from her. I am not a psychologist and not legally qualified to venture into mental health problems, but as a career consultant I did suggest a specific strategy to "break the state of paralysis." When I pointed out that her worry over her son would continue to prevent her from focusing effectively on a new occupation until that problem was resolved, she agreed that I was probably right. Now at least she was dealing with *the right problem*!

Take another look at some of those synonyms for "define" from the *Thesaurus*. Notice that one meaning of "define" is to "set limits", "mark boundaries", or "separate out". In this Lady's situation, several problems seemed to be "lumped together." To locate the "root problem" and solve it meant that first we would have to "separate out" the related problems. Once that was accomplished we were on our way to finding a solution.

The process of "separating out" can be more than a method of defining a problem. It can lead directly to a solution if one is thorough enough in separating out the elements. Let's take the idea of a "problem" itself. Are all problems the same? Do they all bother us equally? Obviously the answer is "no." Let's make a list of problem types by how much they affect us:

- *The worst: Totally overwhelming!*
- *Next worst: You can't stop thinking about it.*
- *Next: It's a constant annoyance but doesn't interfere with activities.*
- *Next: It keeps coming up, but forgotten much of the time.*
- *Next: You only occasionally think of it.*
- *Least: It's a minor problem, hardly worth thinking about.*

Try classifying one of your own problems according to this scale of preoccupation. It helps to put a problem in perspective by just assigning a degree of importance. Is it: *(1) Vitally important to solve! (2) Somewhat important to solve. (3) Relatively unimportant to solve. (4) Not really important to solve at all. Did you notice that you felt you understood the nature of the problem a little better just by classifying it? Perhaps it even made you feel more in control of it.*

When you begin to work on resolving a specific problem, start "defining" it in this manner, using as many tools as you can until the problem begins to feel managable.

Feeling OVERWHELMED by a Problem

My ex-teacher client started out feeling "totally overwhelmed" by her problem situation. When we identified the fact that her relationship with her son was a problem that was *vitally important to solve*, she felt less overwhelmed and more able to focus her energies in that specific direction. Now she could work on a strategy to make solving that problem possible. The next sub-problem was a lack of immediate funds. To resolve her problem with her son she felt she had to go to Hawaii for a while, but she couldn't afford that in her present state of retirement. After a little discussion I learned that the money problem would no longer exist if she resolved the inheritance problem, so that's where I next directed her attention.

One characteristic of "overwhelm" is that it makes a person retreat totally. The dictionary defines "overwhelm" as: *To overcome completely, either physically or emotionally; to overpower.* The result is to leave a person feeling "powerless" and thus totally *stopped*. When either a person or a nation is overcome physically, as in a war or physical combat, the task of rehabilitation can be long and costly. When one has been overwhelmed *emotionally*, however, sometimes the overwhelm can be quite subjective and can gradually fade away. I found that my lady client had become overwhelmed emotionally by the abuse and endless complex demands of her relatives and attorneys. When she realized to what degree it was important for her to get the funds to go to Hawaii to mend her relationship with her son, she found *new inner strength* to fight the inheritance battle. In a relatively short time she resolved the money problem and went to Hawaii. I heard from her several months later and learned that she had indeed renewed a close relationship with her son and found a satisfying occupation to work at not far from where he lived.

Breaking the Problem into Problems and Defining Them

Defining a problem may often require defining several problems, just as solving one problem may require solving several problems. A *Dictionary of Psychology* defines problem solving as *"the process involved in discovering the correct sequence of alternatives leading to a goal."* At times that sequence of alternatives may lead you on a merry chase!

As we progress along in our search for the magic KEY which will unlock your problem or problems, it may be necessary to go beyond these standard definitions. We may have to use a definition which applies very specifically to the problem you are having. In the *Introduction* to this book, I presented eight dimensions of life which relate to eight main divisions of most businesses. In the next chapter you will have an opportunity to define your problem in eight or more different ways, depending on which dimension of your life the problem is mainly affecting. Keep in mind that the KEY which you are searching for will only be the one which works best for you, not everyone. Also it may only unlock one of your problems, but it will begin a process which will enable you to unlock many future doors.

TWO RULES:

Problem creating rule number one:

Always take the narrowest possible view of a problem situation and be certain to shut your eyes and your mind to as many factors and dimensions of the situation as possible.

Problem solving rule number one:

Look at your problem from as many different viewpoints as possible, and define it in many different ways. Notice how other people's problems sometimes seem to you to be easier to solve than your own. Try reversing your viewpoint. Develop the ability to look at your own problems from that outside point of view.

PROBLEM SOLVING POWER
CHECKLIST   NUMBER   THREE

1. **Review:** What is one of the *worst* problems you ever had? Describe it:

2. Did you solve it? If so, how? If not, what happened to it?

3. If you didn't solve that problem, what is the worst problem you have successfully solved? Describe it:

4. Exactly how did you solve it? Describe fully:

5. What problem would you most like to solve at this time? Describe it:

6. One function of defining is "separating out:" Break down your problem into smaller problems. How could you separate out your problem from anything else which might tend to confuse the issue?

7. The dictionary defines a problem as: *A question or situation that presents uncertainty, perplexity or difficulty.* How does your current problem present you with uncertainty? Perplexity? Confusion? Difficulty? *(List all answers for each).*

8. Assign a degree of importance to your problem. Is it: (1) Vitally important to solve?   (2) Somewhat important to solve? (3) Relatively unimportant to solve?   (4) Not really important to solve at all?

9. Compare your present problem to the worst problem your have solved, as described above: Is it easier to solve? Harder? About the same?

10. Defining your problem from a psychological point of view, is there any conflict of thoughts, emotions or other forces? Is any force or element opposing your intent to solve the problem? If so, what?

Note: In defining your problem, did you think of any new ways to approach it? If so add your solution idea to your list at the end of this book. Keep adding to your list of effective problem-solving techniques which work well for you.

Clearly defining a problem allows you to
separate it out from any confusing issues.

4. HOW YOU DEFINE IT IS HOW YOU PERCEIVE IT

OBSERVATION: *Changing the way in which something is defined will change one's perception of it. Defining a problem in a new way will change how that problem is perceived.*

HYPOTHESIS: *Problems remain unsolved because of a failure to take a* total *look at the problem from* every *important viewpoint.*

In today's world we're very status conscious. The clothes we wear, the way we talk, the cars we drive, all *define* who we are in the eyes of many of the people around us. A kid comes down the street with a Mohawk haircut. In today's vernacular, you would probably define him as a "punk rocker" but the kids make finer distinctions than that. Superficially people work backwards. They define people based on how they perceive them. If someone drives a Mercedes, he or she may be *defined* as a "rich person." If it's a BMW, you may define the driver as a "Yuppie."

You also change how you *perceive* people when they are *defined for you:* You see a heavy lady getting out of a car. She looks rather matronly and has a small child with her. At first glance you may *define* her as a "housewife." Then a doorman walks out of the building, comes up to her and says "Let me help you with your niece, Madame President." Suddenly you are confronted with a new view of this woman. Obviously she is someone of far greater importance than you had originally imagined. Had you continued to believe she was a housewife, the chances are you would have interpreted her actions in a way consistent with that viewpoint. Perhaps you would have been a bit disdainful of her weight, or her clumsiness in dealing with the child. Then, when you learned of her true status and her relationship to the child, the odds are you would become more understanding of her lack of familiarity in dealing with the child. Instead of noticing her weight, you would probably notice the fine tailored clothing she was wearing. How she was defined for you would determine, to a great degree, how you would perceive her to be.

Defining Your Own Problem.

Now let's take one of your problems. If my theory is correct, how you define it will determine how you perceive it. Let's start simply. Let's define your problem by degree of difficulty. Is it a "tough" problem? A *very* tough problem? An easy problem? A "normal" problem (whatever that is)? Let's say that you consider it to be a "tough" problem. I assume this means you perceive that it would be quite difficult to solve. Am I right? Write down a description of your problem for me. **STOP** reading right now and take the time to write down that problem. (To gain new skills and ability, you *must* participate in the process. You will gain very little by a passive reading of this book. Don't let this opportunity slip by. Join in the process now. Later you'll be glad you did.)

Look more closely at the problem you wrote down. Watch for words in your description which talk about how difficult the problem is. A typical problem described in one of my workshops was "My car is broken down and I *can't* afford to get it fixed." Notice the word "can't." Another problem: "I can't get my kids to do any work around the house." Once again, notice the word "can't." At the beginning of Chapter 2, I noted all of the synonyms of *"define"* given in a *Thesaurus*. The second definition of *define* has to do with setting boundaries, like defining the exact dimensions of a plot of land. Definitions of words and ideas also set boundaries. Some of the synonyms for *define* were *bound, confine, limit.* The way you *define* a problem can set *definite limitations* on your ability to *solve* it. The word "can't" is probably the *most* limiting word in the English language. A far less limiting (and more truthful) statement would have been, "I have not yet found a workable strategy to resolve my problem."

Try re-writing your problem now, re-stating it in a way that suggests the possibility of a solution. The fellow with the car in need of repair restated his problem as follows: "My car is broken down and I have not yet accumulated the funds to fix it or found a good mechanic who would fix it for less money." This re-statement didn't immediately solve his problem, but it did put it into a more solvable perspective. The lady whose kids wouldn't do work around the house re-stated her problem as follows: "I haven't found a way to communicate with my kids that will get them to willingly do work around the house." In each of these cases, the new definition of the problem pointed in the direction of looking for new skills, additional resources, or new sources of help or information. We might call these more *constructive* definitions, as opposed to *destructive, limiting* definitions, because they open the door to *constructing* more effective avenues to solutions.

Scale and Scope

Observation: *Increasing or decreasing the <u>scale or scope</u> of your problem definition will often lead to new solution possibilities.*

City planners and interior decorators have one thing in common. They're both working with the arrangement of large objects which would require an enormous expenditure of time, money and effort to move around very much. City planners often design the placement of municipal buildings, parks, streets and highways. Interior decorators design the placement of walls, carpets, house plants and furniture. In both cases the only practical way to test the placement of large objects on a grand scale is to *construct a model*. This miniaturization of an entire city or an entire house enables these designers to move small models of large objects about experimentally until they are satisfied with the design on a small scale. They can then translate their design into full-scale streets, buildings or furniture arrangements.

On the other end of the scale, when scientists started working with atomic and sub-atomic particles, they constructed large models of molecular nucleii with the related electrons and protons and neutrons. Similarly designers of the tiny memory chips which operate electronic wrist-watches, pocket calculators, pocket-size radios and micro-cassette recorders first design the circuit boards in a size which is quite visible to the naked eye. That design is then photographically reduced to the size which will be imprinted on the chip.

One of the first steps in getting any problem under control, is illustrating and defining it in a way which is easily grasped by human perception and comprehension.

Defining a Small Organization

In this text I have attempted to state solving techniques broadly, so that you can apply them to any size problem, whether personal, family, business or political. Remember in the *Introduction* I told you that the very minute that you start into any enterprise, even if it's only a lemonade stand, you have created a business structure. You had to have a *production* department to make the lemonade. You had to have the *resources* to make the stand and set it up, and the *financial resources* to have some coins on hand to make change. There had to be some *personnel* to do the work, even if the only person was you. And finally there had to be a *communication and promotion* department to print up a sign that said "Lemonade, two cents a glass."

I noted earlier, that at the age of five or six, you may already have had a business concern with *four* departments: (1) production, (2) resources & finance, (3) personnel, and (4) communication & promotion. In fact, you may have had a few more departments than that. To make the lemonade, you probably had to get a little help from an older brother or sister or your mother. This would have required a little diplomacy and tact, better known in industry as *Public Relations*. This is the department that keeps the company on good terms with the community and *contributes* to Public Service Radio, TV, the Cancer Society, etc. Then you needed the necessary *knowledge* to make the lemonade. In industry that department would be called R & D, *Research & Development*.

Most important of all, I asked you to think about the one department which was there all along, but not noticed because it's so close to home. That is the *executive* department, usually called "Top Management." This is the *prime moving source* of the business. If *you* decided to put together a lemonade stand, *you* were the top executive, the *creative source* of the entire operation.

You may have been surprised to discover that you could have expanded a lemonade stand to *seven* departments, even before you finished kindergarten! If your lemonade stand was successful, you would want to open another stand down the street, and that would mean *expansion*. You would need the eighth department: a department of *marketing expansion* to help you grow effectively. As I said, it's just a *natural* process! Take another look at the diagram of an organization chart with the personal equivalent under each business heading:

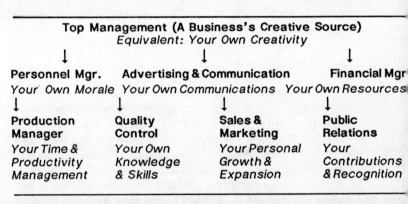

Top Management (A Business's Creative Source)			
Equivalent: Your Own Creativity			
↓	↓		↓
Personnel Mgr.	Advertising & Communication		Financial Mgr
Your Own Morale	*Your Own Communications*		*Your Own Resources*
↓	↓	↓	↓
Production Manager	Quality Control	Sales & Marketing	Public Relations
Your Time & Productivity Management	*Your Own Knowledge & Skills*	*Your Personal Growth & Expansion*	*Your Contributions & Recognition*

Now, looking at one of your problems, see if any of the elements in the following list fits the difficulty you're having:

★ **A creativity problem:** *Frustration with being unable to come up with creative solutions when you need them.*

★ **A mental, physical or emotional morale problem:** *Controlling diet, lack of exercise, insufficient rest or recreation, low energy or self-esteem.*

★ **A communication problem:** *Misunderstandings, upsets, difficulty getting your point across or getting others to* *communicate or listen.*

★ **A financial or lack of resources problem:** *Scarcity of needed cash, capital or other resources.*

★ **A productivity problem:** *Lack of time; failure to finish things; low energy and achievement.*

★ **A knowledge problem:** *Lack of data or technical expertise or skills. Difficulty studying or completing courses of study.*

★ **A growth and expansion problem:** *Dissatisfaction with job or business. Hard to promote or better yourself.*

★ **An exchange of help problem:** *A lack of acknowledgment. Difficulty making a contribution, or receiving recognition for contributions you do make.*

Each type of problem is specifically addressed in a chapter in this book. If your problem fits into one of these departments, take a close look at the chapter that relates to it, and be certain to do the checklist at the end of that chapter very thoroughly.

The Octagon

There is a way you can define each of your problems using a special definition for each of the eight "departments" described above. To make these departments a little more visual, I have organized them into an octagonal (eight-sided) shape (*see illustration*). Octagon means *"having eight angles."* I have provided you with a problem definition for each angle in the octagon. These definitions will give you *eight new angles* to consider as you work through each of your problems. You can use the checklist at the end of this chapter to keep your problem definition process easily organized.

The Definitions:

Resource Definition: Many problems could be viewed as an absence or scarcity of some wanted *resource,* or as an excess of some unwanted "resource." *(Note: Often people or organizations don't solve problems because they don't bring all of the resources at their disposal to bear on the problem).*

Expansion Definition: A problem could be viewed as an obstacle in the path of *growth, development or progress* toward arriving at some projected objective or ideal.

Creativity Definition: A problem could be viewed as a *fixed,* unchanging situation (even if only momentarily) which has not been resolved through usual efforts. The implication is that a new viewpoint, and probably some new innovative action or approach, must be created to *unfix* the situation and resolve the problem.

THE OCTAGON STRATEGIES

OCTAGON: From the Greek, *octagonon*, having eight angles.

STRATEGY: The overall planning and conduct of large-scale combat, political, business or personal operations. A complete problem solving strategy can be structured around the enhancement of each of the following capabilities:

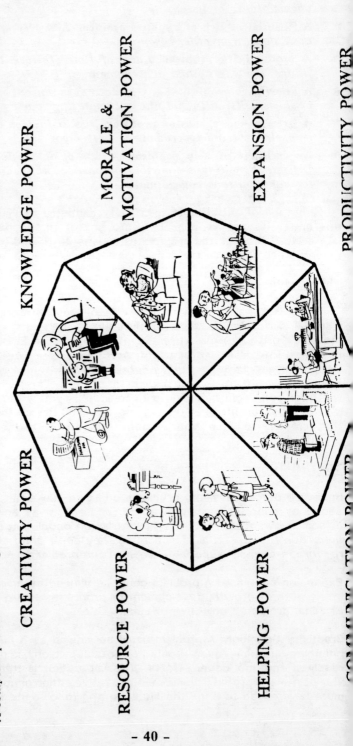

KNOWLEDGE POWER

MORALE &
MOTIVATION POWER

EXPANSION POWER

PRODUCTIVITY POWER

CREATIVITY POWER

RESOURCE POWER

HELPING POWER

Productivity Definition: A problem could be viewed as an obstacle to completing some task or project on the way to reaching a larger objective. It could also indicate a need to increase the speed of productive output.

Knowledge Definition: A problem could be viewed as a situation in which some piece of vital information is either missing or incorrect.

Communication Definition: One definition of communication states that it is *"To be connected or to form a connecting passage."* A problem could be defined as "that which prevents one from *connecting* with a solution." A problem would therefore tend to exist wherever *communication or connecting links* was insufficient or completely missing in an overall situation.

Morale Definition: Many problems reduce to the presence of some *barrier to reaching* what one wishes to be, to do or to obtain. Morale refers specifically to those barriers which are *internal* rather than external. The barrier may cause a lack, like a lack of motivation, enthusiasm, focus or determination. Or the the barrier may be an unwanted presence, such as the presence of unwanted emotions, attitudes or involvements.

(Note: *A problem can usually be defined by the presence or absence of various elements. They may amount to a scarcity or excess of these elements, for example a scarcity of resources, an excess of communication, a scarcity of creativity, an excess of production, etc.)*

Help Definition: Problems generally exist within the context of some exchange between people or between people and things (like machines, the environment, etc.) Where the problem occurs between two or more people, questions of *value, fairness, honesty and concern* become crucial issues. Often a problem breaks down to a question of intent to *help* versus intent to *harm* (or unintentional harm through neglect or irresponsibility.)

Keep in mind that this definition process is just part of the *"input"* step. After you have defined your problem, you will be collecting facts and viewpoints and verifying them (Chapters 6, 7 & 8) before you really begin formulating a solution (Chapter 9).

How One SUPER-SOLVER Defined and Solved Her Problems

Ten years ago Bonnie MacAllister was the first woman ever to receive the SBA's "Small Business Person of the Year" award in the state of Ohio. She also ranked in the top five nationally that same year. Her company, *My Nails, Inc.,* makes and applies artificial fingernails. At the time she received the award she had thirty-six franchise outlets. She started the business in 1975, after she conceived of and had a new chemical formula for artificial nails developed for her.

She had set out to solve the problem of finding a replacement for acrylic nails which were the only ones available at the time. The acrylic nails couldn't tolerate oil or water, the chemical could be absorbed into the human body, and the nails had a foul odor. At this point she had a *knowledge* problem. What substance could serve as a substitute? Bonnie found a chemist who developed a special high-impact polymer for nails which was, as she says, "compatible with, but not harmful to, the body." Perhaps she didn't think of it in these terms, but what she did initially was define her problem as a problem in *creativity.* The basic question she was asking was, "How can we create a nail that will fit these unique specifications?" Because she wasn't a chemist, her next problem could best be called a *resource* problem. Essentially she asked, "Who can I retain to find the chemical formula I need?" Her search led her to the chemist who she calls "A real genius!"

With these initial problems solved and a highly desirable new nail product to market, Bonnie's next project was a *communication* problem. Now she needed to let the world know what she had to offer. She had started her business seriously undercapitalized with only $3000.00. In the beginning she had to focus on word-of-mouth as her only form of advertising, but she instinctively followed Max Gunther's *spider web* formula (the spider who spins the biggest web catches the most flies). With her beautiful blue eyes, a winning smile, high *morale* and contagious enthusiasm she spread the message of her new and exciting "permanent artificial nail" to all of the right people. She had started the business in October and, by May of the following year, the *Columbus Dispatch* had published a generous article on the company and its products. As a result they were swamped with business for the next six months.

Now the main problem became one of *producing* enough of the product to fill orders. Like most small entrepreneurs, Bonnie soon found it was impossible to be in three or four places at once. She had to resolve: How to promote the product sufficiently? How to deliver the product quickly? How to follow through on expansion and marketing plans? And how to accomplish all of this while still keeping a handle on finances and the day-to-day operation of the business? She adopted a solution selected by thousands of small business owners before her: She sought the *help* she needed by tapping some *resources* close to home. Her husband Robert left a job as public relations director for a Cleveland publishing company to help expand the business into a chain of franchises. To get things going, Bonnie and Robert worked twelve-hour days and even recruited their twelve and fourteen year-old sons to help on weekends. Their initial effort to solve an *expansion* problem, was to sell the first franchise for $600.00! As their public relations efforts began to pay off, they raised the price of the franchise to $2000, then $5000, $8000, and, at the time Bonnie received her award, the price was $15,000.

An added dimension of Bonnie's business which keeps it thriving is the attitude that the product is truly *helping* the customer. She says she feels they do more for their customers than ". . . just making their nails look pretty. We make people feel better!" There is a powerful sense of *values* underlying her commercial enterprise. I first realized the power of this values dimension of business when I read *The Art of Japanese Management* in 1981. Authors Richard Pascale and Anthony Athos describe a scene which takes place at 8:00 A.M. all across Japan at installations of the Matsushita Electric Company. Matsushita was the first company in Japan to have a song and a code of values. Every morning 87,000 people recite the code of values and sing together. In the U.S. we would find this behavior silly, but it's hard to argue with the resulting productivity power. Bonnie may not have had her family and employees singing and reciting a code of values, but there is an undeniable presence of her strong values behind her thriving operation.

Not surprisingly, without directly realizing it, Bonnie used all eight of the basic problem solving definitions as she developed her business from a tiny shop, to 36 prosperous franchise outlets. When you apply these definitions to a large, overall development project, it is almost certain you will have an opportunity to use all of the definitions at one time or another. On the other hand, they are equally applicable to small personal goals and projects, even though you may not need all of them. By frequently referring to these definitions, you are less likely to overlook some vital dimension as you attempt to fashion your own business, career or personal endeavor.

Applying the Definitions to Your Own Problem or Problems

In this book, there is a separate chapter devoted to each of the eight dimensions of "the Octagon." As you work through a large project you will probably find that you will encounter problems in about the same order as the related chapters are presented in the book. Nevertheless, you can approach these chapters in any order you choose, just as you selected the checklists you wanted to work on from the KEY Checklist in Chapter One. If your problem is mainly a communication problem, it would be best to go directly to that chapter. If it's a morale problem, then read that chapter next. Choose your own order. Don't feel bound by the arbitrary order I've selected for the chapters. Use the book to fill your own needs and solve your own problems. If it helps you do that, I will feel my efforts have been very well rewarded.

PROBLEM SOLVING POWER

CHECKLIST NUMBER FOUR

Define . . . .

1 - Define your problem in terms of your objective: What is it that this problem is preventing you from being? From doing? From obtaining?

2 - Define your problem in terms of the obstacles: What is standing in the way of you being what you wish to be? Doing what you wish to do? Obtaining what you wish to acquire?

3 - Define your problem in terms of *scarcity* or *lack*: What resource are you lacking that would enable you to overcome the obstacles noted above? If you had access to *unlimited* resources, what resource could you use that would *guarantee* the resolution of your problem?

4 - Define your problem in terms of creativity: What new invention, idea, presentation, activity, connection, environment or other creation would virtually guarantee that you would overcome any obstacles and reach your objective? What is preventing you from creating such an innovative solution?

5 - Define your problem in terms of knowledge: What knowledge, information or skill do you not currently possess which, if you learned or mastered it, would assure the resolution of your problem? What information are you relying on which, if it is false, may be the reason your problem is persisting? How can you check the accuracy of this information?

6 - Define your problem in terms of personal morale and motivation: Are you experiencing any emotion or attitude which makes you feel hopeless or powerless to solve your problem? Have you felt this way in the past? Is there someone who reminds you of this past feeling or attitude? Is there something which would motivate you so strongly that you could resolve your problem despite any pessimistic attitudes, painful emotions, or negative influences?

7 - Define your problem in terms of help versus harm: Is there some person or group you wish to help by solving this problem? Is there some person or group who could help you solve it? Is there some person or group who would be harmed if you solved this problem? Is there someone who is actively preventing you from solving the problem?

8 - Define your problem in terms of communication: Is there some person or group you cannot easily communicate with, which is contributing to the continuation of your problem? If you could communicate *anything* to *anyone* with no consequences, what could you communicate that would begin to resolve your problem?

9 - Define your problem in terms of productive action: Is there some obstacle in the way of your completing those actions which would resolve your problem? Is there a lack of time to try various solutions to your problem? Is there some handicap or limitation keeping you from speeding up your problem-solving activities?

10 -Define your problem in terms of expansion: How is this problem an obstacle in the path of your growth and development toward your larger objectives in life? Is the problem barring your expansion into new spaces, new environments, new marketplaces, or new activities?

"Many people would sooner die than think. In fact they do."
—Bertrand Russell

THINK *v.* **1.** *To have as a thought; formulate in the mind.* **2.** *To reason about or reflect on; ponder. To decide by thinking.* **3.** *To judge or regard.* **4.** *To believe; suppose.* **5.** *To expect; anticipate.* **6.** *To remember; call to mind.* **7.** *To visualize; imagine.* **8.** *To devise or invent.*

*The scars of loss and victimization are not
easily erased,   but the past must be
dismissed for the present to flourish.*

5. MORALE & MOTIVATION POWER

"If you aren't fired with enthusiasm,
you will be fired with enthusiasm."

—*Vince Lombardi*

Morale: *1. The state of the spirits of an individual or group, as shown in confidence, cheerfulness, discipline and willingness to perform selected or assigned tasks.*

Hypothesis: *Any problem can be solved with sufficient motivation and high morale.*

In the introduction to this book, I mentioned several very successful people who are prime examples of effective problem solvers. All of these successful individuals possess the ability to maintain a high morale. Looking at the lives of these people, I asked myself, what are the common denominators? What are the ingredients that make up "high morale"? The best list of qualities I have heard were presented by Ken Blanchard, author of the best selling *One Minute Manager,* at a major *Toastmasters International* conference. Ken called his ingredients "The Five P's of Performance": *purpose, pride, patience, persistence* and *perspective.* These are definitely the morale building qualities that the problem-solvers I selected had in common.

Purposes, Aspirations and Motivation

The enemies of high morale are fear, doubt, uncertainty, anxiety, resentment, regret and apathy. Only a powerful purpose will motivate a person to press on through these negative emotions to reach his or her highest purposes and aspirations. Fred A. Dyer, vice-president and director of marketing for a major health maintainance organization, was a regular attendee and an enthusiastic supporter of my first problem solving workshops. During one workshop, Fred perfectly summed up the role of *purpose* in problem solving. He said, "If your desire to reach your objective is greater than your fear of facing the obstacles, you'll face them and go for it." Public speaking is a prime example of this circumstance. It has been said that the fear of speaking is public is greater for most people than the fear of death! Nevertheless many people must overcome their fear and master the art of speaking in front of groups to reach their career objectives. Fred and I both joined a local Toastmasters club in the late 1970s, for this very same reason.

Most of the people in the club we joined, needed to speak in the context of their jobs. They were making sales presentations, teaching workshops, presenting corporate speeches, giving political speeches or, like some attorneys and judges in our group, addressing the ladies and gentlemen of the jury. We all had two things in common: (1) When we got up in front of a group to speak we were nervous, uncertain and often unimaginative and uninteresting, and (2) we were strongly *motivated* to overcome these problems and to become competent speakers so we could perform and prosper in our various careers. Our motivation was greater than our fears, doubts, uncertainties and anxieties, and so we persisted until every one of us became, at the very least, a competent speaker.

Super solvers take the *purpose* dimension of morale one step further, however. Ed Morler is a close personal friend who delivers negotiating skills seminars to top negotiating personnel in major banks, corporations and governments. Effectively focusing on *purpose* is number one on Ed's list of vital negotiating skills. Many times in the course of a seminar Ed will say, "Don't assume that your aspirations are high enough; *high aspirations win more!*" He proves his point over and over as attendees at his workshops participate in role-plays where they must negotiate for multi-million dollar properties, companies or commodities and often fall far short of a good deal. The best negotiators are those who start out with a good grasp of how high their opening demands can be without appearing so ridiculous that no one would enter into negotiations with them, but ridiculous enough to give ample room for concessions while obtaining an excellent deal. Olympic athletes who have broken records have set goals of new highs which would have seemed ridiculous and unattainable to those who set earlier records. Those higher aspirations have motivated them to break the limitation barrier. Super solvers are those who take on "ridiculous" problems which others have long ago abandoned as unsolvable. They watch for "doors of opportunity" which will allow them to make new breakthroughs and set "ridiculous" new records.

Super-Solver Morale Creates Opportunities

One of my favorite *super-solvers* is Cal ("Go see Cal") Worthington who, as I mentioned earlier, is the nation's largest car dealer, selling cars to over a quarter million people every year. Cal has been an innovative problem solver since the day he quit school to go to work for the CCC (Civilian Conservation Corps). When the second world war broke out, Cal, with only seven years of formal education, wanted to become a pilot in the Army Air Corps. The Air Corps required two years of college and Cal didn't even come close. Cal's problem seemed unsolveable, but then a door of opportunity opened up. The Air Corps became desperate for pilots and changed the policy to accept an equivalency examination for two years of college. While he was in the CCC, Cal read books constantly. He easily passed the examination and became a top-notch pilot with many medals to his credit by the end of the war.

After the war Cal expected to find a pilot's job with a commercial airline, but they all required a college degree. Cal's financial condition soon became so desperate he had to sell his car. He polished it up and took it to the local post office to show it off. Within a couple of hours the car was sold. A couple of months later he bought another car and sold that one at a good profit also. From that point forward, Cal's aspirations and motivation grew constantly. With little more than determination to build on, he rented a small lot, fixed up five old cars and sold them in less than a week. He was in business. The next hurdle was higher. After several years he was still just one of many small dealers. Even when TV advertising came in, his commercials were pretty much like every other car dealer's. How to jump that hurdle of mediocrity was his problem. How could he stand out in the crowd and capture the lion's share of the market?

Cal's next door of opportunity opened when a competitor introduced his pet dog into his commercials with him. Cal figured he could go that one better with ease. He introduced his dog "Spot," only Spot wasn't a dog. It was a gorilla. Cal finally got people's attention. His offbeat sense of humor plus his cowboy clothes and manner of speaking appealed to people and they began coming in and buying cars. After that people could never tell what Cal's "Dog Spot" might be next. It could be anything from a gopher to an elephant. What never changed was Cal's sense of humor and his willingness to do whatever he had to to get people's attention, even if it meant walking on the wing of his plane to prove he could "beat any deal." Ten years ago Cal had five dealerships but he was projecting anywhere from twenty to forty dealerships. Once he found out how high he could fly, he never lacked "high aspirations."

Patience and Persistence

Patience and persistence seem to follow naturally from a well-focused sense of purpose. All of the *super-solvers* I have studied never let up on their persistence to arrive at their objectives, but they also retained a sense of patience when they saw that some things simply could not be pushed beyond a certain point. R. David Thomas went on from creating the *Kentucky Fried Chicken* image for Colonel Sanders, to creating the *Wendy's Old Fashioned Hamburgers* chain from the bottom up. He says it took four years of very

long hours and patient attention to detail to get the business off
the ground, but he knew where he was going and how to get there.
With that kind of *certainty of purpose,* problems get solved and
morale never becomes a problem.

Pride, Self-Respect. Courage and Priorities

In problem-solving workshops I am often asked, "When you
have a tough problem, why does it always seem you're going around
in circles when you try to start solving it?" To answer that question
its necessary to look at the six worsening phases one passes through,
moving down from the onset of a problem, to the point where
one completely gives up on trying to solve it. Each phase presents
the problem-plagued individual with an opportunity to break out
of this worsening pattern. There are two qualities needed, at each
step along the way, to break out of the declining pattern: (1) The
courage to face the problem at that point, and (2) the determination
to resolve it.

You may recognize some familiar phenomena as you read through
these phases. I believe you will see why anything less than total
commitment to finding a solution can leave you "running around
in circles" in any of these phases.

1.   *Phase one:* An unpleasant problem situation arises. It can
      be as simple as having to return some merchandise to a store
      or as terribly unpleasant as admitting that you damaged some-
      one's car, office machine, or other property. It can also be
      as extreme as having to fire someone or, like several of the
      Presidents of our country, having to tell the nation the truth
      about some scandal within the government administration. The
      common denominator is the fact that *one does not wish to
      face up to this unpleasant situation.* (If one faces the problem
      immediately, it can be handled quickly and is not likely to
      get worse.)

2.   If the problem isn't handled in phase one, in phase two, there
      are several factors which tend to make it get worse. The first
      is *procrastination:* putting the problem off to deal with
      later—usually at some indefinite, nebulous point in the distant
      future. This can be coupled with concern about "saving face."
      (Many politicians have been caught in this trap. Few have
      gotten out gracefully.) Another factor is an inherent element
      of *withdrawal* from the problem situation, which, translated
      into military terms, equates with "retreat." This is a little

like backing down from an angry dog. If you turn and run, it is likely to chase you. Winston Churchill said: *"One ought never to turn one's back on a threatened danger and try to run away from it. If you do that you will double the danger. But if you meet it promptly and without flinching, you will reduce the danger by half. Never run away from anything—NEVER!"*

There is an additional liability to phase two. In the process of shutting the problem out from one's mind and withdrawing, a portion of one's mind and attention has also been shut out. This reduces the amount of awareness and alertness one has available to focus on other problems at hand. The resulting liability thus increases the likelihood of *accumulating additional unsolved problems.* Once one is pulled into this toilet-flush, downward spiral, reversing the trend and moving back in a positive direction will require much more determination than would have been needed had the problem been addressed in phase one. The treacherousness of this situation completely dictates the selection of your TOP PRIORITY ACTION:

Your first priority in resolving a problem should be to do that which frees your attention from nagging concerns, thus allowing you to focus your FULL attention on the major issues of the problem.

3. By the time you reach phase three, the problem has been around a while. Facing up to it and trying to solve it has been postponed. Any attempt to think about the problem will now result in feeling *very confused.* A vivid picture may help to illustrate this phenomenon: Imagine a tornado rushing across the ground somewhere on the plains of Kansas or Oklahoma (if you haven't experienced one in the flesh), flattening houses and tearing up entire trees as it goes. Now imagine that you are there and you have ducked into a storm cellar to escape the deadly force of the wind. Every time you stick your head out, you encounter the rushing chaos of that wind and so you duck back down.

The chaos of the tornado is symbolic of the unpleasantness of the problem you have to face. Procrastinating, backing down and retreating is like ducking into the storm cellar. Now to get out of the cellar you must go up through that *zone of chaos* surrounding the problem. That is the feeling of confusion you encounter when you try to think about the problem. Unlike facing a tornado, you can face the confusion of most problems without being physically destroyed. The sooner you do so, the sooner you will be able to get up out of whatever mental and emotional cellar you have allowed yourself to become trapped in.

4. In phase four, you have chosen to remain in the cellar, completely hiding from the problem and its torrent of confusion. This phase is one of self-condemnation, self-disparagement and loss of self-respect, although these feelings may be disguised with a false bravado. Real pride, as Ken Blanchard calls the state of healthy self-respect, has flown out the window. The best way to restore it, of course, is to work back up through these phases and to face up to that confusion. You must do whatever it takes to solve the problem. When it is solved, self-respect will return.

5. In phase five the problem has been allowed to remain for a *very* long time. At this point it has begun to serve as a *nucleus* or a magnet, and it is attracting many additional problems which then become attached to that nucleus. You will recall the Watergate scandal when President Nixon did what he called "stone-walling" to avoid confronting and talking to the press. Many other problems in his administration, which may have gone unnoticed under other circumstances, became serious issues. When he lost the trust of the American people and Congress, it became impossible for him to get the legislation he wanted passed. The press attacked him constantly, and you can be certain he had other personal and physical problems which arose as a direct result of those attacks. *Problems tend to attract more problems.* Fortunately, *solutions also tend to generate more solutions.* When one finally begins to face up to a problem, or a series of problems, as each one is resolved there seems to be more *momentum* toward the resolution of the remaining problems.

6. In phase six, there is a blurring of exactly what the problem is. Often the result is a perpetual state of low self-respect and poor morale, with no specific reason clearly in sight. The accumulation of uresolved problems has reached a point of "critical mass." There are so many problems, you simply "don't know where to start." If you had to wait until *all* of the problems were resolved before you could restore a sense of pride and self-respect, it would probably never happen. A more workable strategy would be to *restore the sense of pride and self-respect first,* in any way that you can. With an improved state of morale, most people can solve any problem more quickly and easily. Regardless of the state you're in,

it would be useful to ask yourself every day: "What could I do today that would make me feel better about myself?" You might also follow that with, "What could I do today, for someone else, that would make me feel I was more capable of contributing to the good of my fellow man?"

This last point can be of great value, if you are able to apply it. Self-worth and self-respect are concepts which mainly relate to your dealings with other people. When someone cares about you and is concerned about you, you consider that person to be "worthwhile." When we go through life, bestowing attention and concern and appreciation on others, we become a *source* of good feelings for those individuals. Think about that for a moment. That is quite a lot of power to possess. With a sincerely kind word you can often lift another person's spirits. You can actually *improve their morale!* When you are able to view yourself as a *source of power* for others, your own sense of self-worth will soar!

Negative Emotions Usually Connect to the Past

At the beginning of this chapter I pointed out that the enemies of high morale and motivation are fear, doubt, uncertainty, anxiety, resentment, regret and apathy. As my friend, Fred Dyer, pointed out: *Only a powerful purpose will motivate a person to press on through these negative emotions to reach his or her highest purposes and aspirations.* Rather than having to press on through these emotions and resistances, it would obviously be better to simply *remove them* if that were possible. Initially I have focused on ways for you to *motivate yourself* strongly enough to push through any barrier or wall of negative emotions or attitudes. Professional help is often needed to *eliminate* these inner barriers, but this can be an expensive process, and will not be pursued by everyone. Recurring or inappropriate negative emotions are often rooted in the past, in traumatic childhood, teen-age, and early adult experiences. These experiences often involve failure, pain, rejection or even violence. Psychotherapy is usually necessary to remove or resolve the scars of such traumatic experiences, and competent professional help should be sought if these emotions are so powerful that you cannot overcome them alone.

Since you are capable of reading this book, it is unlikely that you have emotional scars which run so deep that you cannot work through them to obtain what you want out of life. People who read self-help books are already motivated to make changes in their lives. Nevertheless, it will be helpful for you to *recognize* when a negative emotion or attitude is rooted in the past. That recognition will better enable you to do everything possible to reduce or eliminate its power over your ability to resolve problems in the present. To focus fully on resolving a problem in the here and now, you cannot have part of your attention and energy focused or locked up in some past, unresolved problem. To write a new chapter in your life, often you first have to:

CLEAN THE SLATE!

You want to identify earlier problems you have had which have been similar in some way to the problem you are now having. You can benefit from this in three ways:

1. If you can identify which of those problems you successfully solved, you may be able to apply some variation of that solution again in your present situation.

2. If you can identify which of those problems remains unsolved, perhaps you can identify what you would have done *differently* in the light of what you know now, and save yourself from making a similar mistake in the present.

3. If you can identify any of those problems which still plague you as an unfinished dimension of your past, you may now be able to either resolve them or completely terminate them so they no longer rob you of attention, energy, and enthusiasm for life.

Putting LABELS on the Past

To get a better idea of how the past can intrude on your present, do a brief inventory of past problems you have had which have been similar in some way to the problem you have now. Instead of writing each problem out in great detail, a better approach would be to *draw* a "time line" across the top of a piece of paper, from left to right. This can represent the years of your life, ending right now in the present at the far right end of the line. Next, write a LABEL which describes, in a word or two, the problem you are now having. Put this at the end of your time line in the zone which represents the present. Then go back along your time line to a point when you had a similar problem. Make another brief two-or-three-word LABEL at that point also. Next work backwards along that time line, putting LABELS wherever you had some sort of related problem. Continue back along your time line until you have LABELLED all of the earlier problems you could recall.

I asked you to make your time line across the top of the paper so you could put additional information in a column below each experience LABEL. Start with the LABEL you wrote to describe your present problem. Write beneath it a list of the *emotions* and *attitudes* you have, which are somewhat of a barrier to your solving the problem. Then beneath each of the other problem LABELS on your time line, write the emotions and attitudes which were connected with that earlier experience, until you have a list under each of the LABELS (*see sample illustration.*)

Time Line Example

May, 1970	July, 1975	Jan., 1981	June, 1985	Dec., 1988
What happened?				
Failed HS math	Quit college	Layed off	Demoted on job	Lost job
Emotions and attitudes:				
Confusion	Despair	Anger	Rage	Anger
Frustration	Anger	Confusion	Frustration	Frustration
Indifference	Sadness	Frustration	Despair	Confusion
Incomplete Actions:				
Letter to HS	Letter to Dean	Letter to ex-boss	Request details	New job application
DUMP IT	DO IT NOW	DUMP IT	DO MONDAY	DO IT NOW

Next take one of the emotions or attitudes in your present problem list and CIRCLE it. Then look back at the list under each of the other labels, and CIRCLE that same attitude or emotion, if it is there. When you have finished CIRCLING those items, draw a *connecting line* from the list under the present LABEL, back along the time line, from circle to circle, to the earliest one. Then do the same CIRCLING process with *each of the emotions and attitudes* under the present problem list, *drawing a line to connect it* to the same emotions and attitudes under the other LABELS. When you finish you should have a very visual picture of how your present feelings connect to your earlier problems.

Handling Some Unfinished Business

For most people it's difficult to begin working on a new project when they haven't finished an old one. Around the house I may still be working on a summer yard project when fall comes and it's time to begin getting the house ready for winter weather. Reluctantly, I put aside the summer project to begin the winter preparation tasks, but I would feel better about doing them if I had finished the summer projects first.

Most people's lives are full of abandoned and unfinished tasks and projects. Garages and attics are filled with half-sewn clothes, half-built bookshelves and half-finished jigsaw puzzles. Clearing these out can be a simple matter if you have the *will to admit* that you will probably never finish the project and the *willingness to throw out* the unfinished item. It is mostly a simple matter of making a decision. Decide whether or not you're going to finish it. Then either do it or get rid of it. In business they often refer to the "four D's": DO IT, DELEGATE IT, DELAY IT OR DUMP IT. A word of warning, however. If you decide to *delay it again,* now that you have reviewed a task, put a "time tag" on it. Note *exactly when* you will come back and finish it, or note a time when you will absolutely know it's hopeless and should be DUMPED.

The same process can be effective with old problems and unfinished intentions. Go back to your time line and your column lists under the problem LABELS. This time, in just a word or two, under your previous lists, add a list of *unfinished actions.* Note down if you never sent a thank you note or other communication. Note any legal actions you didn't finish, like filing taxes, legally terminating a contract or business relationship, or paying some fee or fine. Recalling this unfinished business may not come easily. Stick with it. Go from column to column, adding a little to each list until you feel you have completed them. (see illustration) If you think of something to add to a list later, feel free to come back and add to your lists any time you like. The important thing is to feel you have *taken these unfinished items out of your mind and put them down onto the paper!*

Now use the "four D's." Go through your lists and note whether you will (1) Do it now, (2) Delegate it and get someone else to do it, (3) Delay action until a very specific future date, or (4) Dump it, that is decide to completely end this unfinished business right now and never think about it again. If you are effective at carrying out this process, you should feel like you are able to begin working on your present problem with renewed vigor. You have cleaned the slate and now you can write a new experience on your chalkboard of life without the intrusion of lingering phantoms from the past.

Defining and Dealing with Morale Problems

Many problems reduce to the presence of some *barrier to reaching* what one wishes to be, to do or to obtain. Morale refers specifically to those barriers which are *internal* rather than external. The barrier may cause a lack, like a lack of motivation, enthusiasm, focus or determination. Or the the barrier may be an unwanted presence, such as the presence of unwanted emotions, attitudes or involvements.

There are two distinct ways in which morale can be a problem. One is when your own morale is low, and the other when the morale of people on whom you depend is low. When your own morale is low, problems often look larger than they are. A very gifted teacher I had in college once said, "If you make the problem larger than yourself, you'll *never* be able to solve it." When your sense of self-worth, dignity and self-respect becomes low, you feel small. Even a minor problem can loom over you like a towering mountain. It can feel *totally* overwhelming. At that point it is vital to do whatever you can to raise your morale. When your family members, employees or business associates fall into this state of low morale, they can become problem-*creators* rather than problem-*solvers!* If this happens, their problems can easily become *your* problems. Don't fall into this trap. Your best strategy is to raise their morale so that *they can solve their own problems! There are some very specific measures you can take to accomplish this task.*

Joy Wright is president of Profile Systems, Inc., a personnel consulting firm in Bedford, Texas. She is an occasional contributor to *The Typographer*, the trade paper published by the Typographic International Association. In the 1988 Spring edition of the paper, she contributed an article entitled, *Poor Morale, a Hidden Cost Factor.* The article caught my eye because I rarely see the problem of poor morale addressed so directly. Joy points out that turnover and training costs can range from $5000 to $20,000 per employee depending on position and technical skill. What she also points out (which is often ignored), is that the loss of an employee due to a morale problem costs much more because of the *disruption* to other employees. *Poor morale is contagious.* Often when one employee quits, others will follow.

Looking over Joy's list of factors *causing* poor morale, I was struck by how well they fitted into the octagon pattern. The items pointed clearly to corrective measures which would increase the morale of any working group:

* *Resources:* Poor materials, equipment or working environment.
* *Creativity:* Lack of recognition or feedback for creative ideas, suggestions and innovations.
* *Knowledge:* Lack of employee orientation or training; lack of sales, management or job training.
* *Motivation:* Poor benefits, poor pay and lack of incentives. A lack of regular performance or salary reviews.
* *Help:* Lack of team effort.

- *Communication:* Major breakdown in this area: No distribution of regular information through notice boards, memos or departmental meetings; uncertainty about where to direct communication because of a lack of established chain of command or organization chart.

- *Production:* No organized approach to production schedules; no standard job descriptions; no established policies and procedures.

- *Expansion:* No sales training or involving of all employees in a marketing expansion viewpoint; no rewards or incentives for special efforts to contribute to the company's market growth and expansion.

Joy notes further that the KEY critical factor behind poor morale is *poor management personality.* In this particular industry she found that production-oriented managers often forced projects through to meet deadlines, while providing little feedback or recognition to employees.

During the same week in April, 1988, when I saw this article on morale, a friend handed me a clipping from the *Wall Street Journal,* entitled "Five Main Reasons Why Managers Fail." The number five reason was: "unable to rebound." Number four was: "fear of action." Number three: "the me-only syndrome." Number two was "failure to adapt." And what was number one? *"Inability to get along!"* The article points out:

> Poor interpersonal skills represent the single biggest reason for failure—especially in the early and middle stages of a manager's career—and the most crucial flaw to recognize and remedy.

> For some the problem is getting along with subordinates. Managers typically can't inspire and win the loyalty of underlings because they aren't good listeners. They don't give and take criticism well and "view conflict as something bad instead of something inevitable that has to be handled," says Robert Lefton, president of Psychological Consultants, Inc., a consulting firm in St. Louis, MO.

I believe the best advice on creating an atmosphere of high morale where problems get solved effectively by subordinates, was given by J. William Grimes, the head of the ESPN sports television cable network. A *Success* magazine article reports that Grimes always allows his subordinates to *make major decisions* rather than reserving that role for himself. It is his belief that the sense of responsibility and pride this power gives them is worth the price of an occasional mistake. At one point he allowed a young head of programming and production to televise the America's Cup live—at *midnight* against his own objections. The cost was $2 million! Amazingly, it was so successful the profit was $2 million!

Grimes relates that he mastered the art of management at CBS where he rose to a vice presidency by the age of thirty. He says he learned all of the wrong things to do by being an employee with ineffective bosses. In his view, motivating employees comes down to one simple rule: *Make them feel that their opinions really count!* It's the old *ownership* rule. When people borrow or rent houses or cars, they often abuse them. What they *own*, they will more likely treat with great care. Delegated authority follows the same rule. When you really own it, you give it all you've got. Grimes believes you should give people *real autonomy;* make sure they stay motivated and quickly *get rid of those who lack motivation.* That is the key to maintaining great morale!

To Build Morale, Take a Look at the Other Guy

I opened this chapter with Ken Blanchard's five "P"s of performance: *purpose, pride, patience, persistence* and *perspective.* All of these qualities are crucial to building good morale, but *perspective* is often least emphasized. A much over-used story tells of the man who was depressed because he had no shoes until he saw the man who had no feet. The story may be a tired cliche, but it illustrates perfectly the value to be gained in comparing your problem to others whose problems are far more serious.

If you have fallen into a low state of morale over an inability to resolve a longstanding problem, get some perspective on the situation by doing the following:

1. Write down your problem.
2. Write down a list of problems which would be equally as bad, but no worse.
3. Write down a list of problems which would be far worse than yours.
4. Write down several problems which you would rather have.
5. Repeat steps one through four until you notice a positive change in how you feel about your situation.

If this doesn't cure your poor morale and improve your outlook, do the following: Take a trip to one of the poor sections of town. Notice people who look troubled and write down what you *imagine* their problems to be (or ask them, if you feel you could handle that). Then notice people living in that same area of poverty, who nevertheless seem cheerful and problem-free. Ask yourself how these people must be viewing life to have such a high morale in this environment.

Then consider how you might emulate their behavior to raise your own morale in your present situation. You may have to make a change in your life. To solve any problem, you must change something. If you fear change, no solution is possible. Use your problems to motivate you to make constructive changes.

If you succeed in raising your own morale, you may find that many of your problems have somehow vanished when you weren't looking.

PROBLEM SOLVING POWER
C H E C K L I S T   N U M B E R   F I V E

1 - **(Revise)** In regard to your problem, what could you do to raise your aspirations higher?

2 - What purpose could motivate you so intensely, that you could easily face any fear, anxiety, doubt or other negative attitude or emotion which might arise while you are trying to solve your problem?

3 - Have you been less persistent than you might have in trying to solve this problem? Or have you become impatient? How could you increase your determination to persist once again?

4 - What could you do today or this week to increase your feeling of pride and self-respect in regard to this problem?

5 - Have you backed down or been less than courageous in dealing with this problem situation? How might you summon up more courage and face up to whatever unpleasant circumstances you have to handle? Who or what could help you?

6 - Can you think of someone who has had a similar problem to yours? If so, contact that person and have him or her tell you about that problem and attempted solutions. Be understanding and listen. Do not offer advice or discuss *your own* problem!

7 - Do you know of someone who has a much worse problem than yours? To gain perspective, contact this person and have him or her tell you about the problem. Once again, be understanding and listen. Do not offer advice. Do not discuss *your* problem at any length. Just listen.

8 - Do you know of someone who has had a similar problem to yours (or worse), and solved it? If so, contact that person and have him or her tell you about the problem, how it occurred and how it was solved. Take notes but do not ask for specific advice.

9 - Look into books, tapes, classes, workshops or courses which are designed to increase self-esteem, raise morale and inspire motivation. While you are working on this problem situation, try to fit one or more morale-raising training programs into your schedule.

10 -Make a list of activities which could raise your spirits and overall morale. Work out a way to engage in one of those activities every week while you are resolving this problem. The lift in morale will strengthen your ability to deal with your problem and to attract more supportive help.

Collecting and verifying information is the first vital step in problem solving.

6. "KNOWLEDGE IS POWER"
Francis Bacon, 1597

Knowledge: *1. The state or fact of knowing. 2. Familiarity, awareness or understanding gained through experience or studyy 3. That which is known; the sum or range of what has been perceived, discovered or inferred. 4. Learning; erudition. 5. Specific information about something.*

Special Definition: *A problem could be viewed as a troublesome situation in which some piece of vital information is either missing or incorrect.*

Hypothesis: *Any problem can be solved with sufficient knowledge.*

In a previous chapter, I introduced you to the phases of problem solving:

  INPUT   VERIFY   DESIGN   TEST   APPLY

In giving talks on problem solving to various groups, I often ask for a show of hands on which of these five main categories people believe are most often not handled properly, with the result that problems go unsolved. Which do you think most people selected? Solution design? Many people choose that category but, no. Even more choose "Apply." People believe that problems aren't solved because the solutions aren't applied properly. That does happen, of course, but that is not the *main* reason problems go unsolved. The phase of problem solving which is most neglected, which causes the vast majority of unsolved problems, is *input!* Input is frequently insufficient, incomplete and inadequate!

"Input" includes a *recognition* of exactly what the problem is all about. In the previous chapter you were given many different ways to define your problem. Picture a big stewing pot to represent the "input" phase of problem-solving. In that pot you're going to put all of the ingredients of the problem, just as though you were putting a mix of meat and vegetables and seasonings into a stew. Your ingredients will include your own viewpoint of the problem, the viewpoints of others, structured information like the rules you're learning from this book plus all of the specific facts of the problem situation.

When you think of "input," you may simply think of the overall process of collecting information, but this step encompasses far more than that. The "input" step can include:

- Getting everyone involved in the problem situation to tell yo exactly what they perceive the problem to be and what the believe should be done to solve it.

- Finding out exactly what other information is needed to resolv the problem, and then finding out where that knowledge migh be obtained. It may be necessay to connect up to a universit data base, to contact a specialized consultant, or even t take specialized college courses to obtain the informatio needed.

- Looking in trade magazines, specialized reference books or periodical review of magazines and publications. You can ofte turn up other people who have had similar problems. You ca then find out how they solved them.

- Talking to competitors, rivals or other people in a simila circumstance or business situation, to find out directly if the have had a similar problem and if so how they solved it.

- Surveying suppliers, employees, contract services, customer and perhaps even prospective customers, to find out the reaction to the problem and possible solutions you might try Solutions which offend people on whom you depend for surviv could create even bigger problems. It's best to get this inpu before taking any action.

- Checking with city, state or even federal authorities to fin out if there are any restrictions you have to consider whe formulating a solution. You may even have to do your ow environmental impact study.

- Gathering information on the physical and mental stability c people who may be affected by various solutions to the problem Solutions which make other people angry, uncomfortable c even sick will only create larger problems. Often it's necessar to do a kind of "human impact study" before deciding on ar implementing a solution.

As you can see, collecting "input" is quite a job, but the solutic may become obvious while you are doing this input step. It ma then be unnecessay to spend any more time on the problem-solvir process. Sometimes it's not even necessary to *do* anything about th problem. The very process of asking for information and listenir to the answers can bring about a solution in itself. Especially if tl person collecting the input is a *good listener.* The chapter on *Commu. ication Power* deals with this vital aspect of the "input" step. L Iacocco achieved fame by turning around the fortunes of the Chrysl Corporation when it was on the ropes. He says one of his most powerf assets was an ability to listen and to communicate. For informatic input and application output to be complete and effective, skillf communication is the KEY ability.

Just the Facts, Ma'am

Fact: *1. Something known with certainty. 3. Something that has been objectively verified. 4.Something having real,demonstrable existence.*

Conjecture: *1. Inference based on inconclusive or incomplete evidence; guesswork. 2. An opinion or conclusion based on inference.*

Assumption: *2. A statement accepted or supposed true without proof or demonstration.*

The collecting of viewpoints, ideas and opinions provides helpful input, but the most essential input is that which you can rely upon with *certainty*. In a court of law, your opponent's attorney will be quick to challenge *conjectures*. You may be advised by the judge to, "stick to the facts." Conjecturing can be a way of jumping to conclusions before all of the evidence is in. Juries are advised not to accept conjectures or to jump to conclusions. You would be well advised to follow the same rule.

It is common for problems to arise around disagreements, misunderstandings, errors or disputes over finances. I'm sure you've experienced this yourself. An argument can be quickly settled when the facts of the matter are revealed, if it is a disgreement over facts rather than opinions. Computers have saved business owners and managers many thousands of dollars and much anxiety and frustration, by providing detailed factual information. At a moment's notice you can have details on inventory, sales, personnel performance, and financial investments. Reliable information makes the solving of any problem an easier task.

It is also possible to use facts as powerful sales and persuasion tools. In 1977, Stephen King, the famous author of modern horror stories, was negotiating a new contract with Doubleday & Co. They had paid him only $29,000 for his first three books. Kirby McCauley was a writer's agent who at that point had sold only a few previously unsalable short stories for King. But King was impressed with his *knowledge* of the industry and his attention to detail in matters like obtaining proper copyright protection. When King asked Doubleday for $800,000 for three books and they told him "to go to hell," he asked McCauley to get involved. McCauley moved King from Doubleday to Viking Press (for hardcover), and New American Library (for paperback.) King says that when McCauley negotiated the Viking contract for him, he became rich. His first book for Viking, *The Dead Zone*, sold two and a half times more copies than his last one for Doubleday.

During the last couple of years McCauley made two of the biggest

deals in publishing history: $10 million for two books by Ki
and $1.7 million for a book by the late Frank Herbert of *Dune* fan
McCauley says, "My style is not hard sell. I just present the fa
the way they are."

"Trust But Verify"
Russian saying quoted by Ronald Reagan

Verify: *1. To prove the truth of by the presentation of eviden
or testimony; to substantiate. 2. To determine or test the tru
or accuracy of, as by comparison, investigation or reference.*

As this chapter was being written in 1987, President Reagan h
just completed a series of talks with Mikhail Gorbachev, the curr
Soviet leader. New arms control measures were agreed upon. Beca
of the Soviet's long-standing practice of violating arms control agr
ments, Reagan often referred to an old Russian proverb: "Trust l
verify." This warning should also be heeded by any problem sol
who sets out to "learn the facts" of a problem situation.

Problems in government serve as examples of why verificatior
so vital. Earlier in 1987, hearings were conducted to "learn the fac
surrounding a government scandal called "Iranscam," wherein fui
collected from Iran for arms the U.S. Government secretly sold t
country, were secretly diverted to support "Contra" rebels in Nicarag
In the course of these hearings, as in the Watergate hearings of
Nixon era, many facts were hidden or distorted so that truth
very difficult to determine. People under pressure learn at a very ea
age that the easiest way out of many situations is to lie. If the prob
you are trying to solve is being *created* by the actions of some
involved in the problem situation, it is highly unlikely that per
will tell you the truth when asked.

The most fundamental rule of problem solving comes from
solving of a simple arithmetic addition problem: *If the numb
in the column being totaled are not correct, the sum of th
numbers will also be wrong.* Put into more personal terms, if
enter the amount of a check in your checkbook incorrectly, when
go to determine your balance, the numbers will not add up correc
One of the most essential functions you will perform as a prob
solver is to *verify that the facts you are collecting are true.*

"How," you may ask, "can I determine if someone is telling
truth?" The simplest way is to get the story or the facts from
and preferably three or more sources. Tape record verbal account
you can check back on small details. Then you can compare the sto
and see if there is a discrepancy between them. In financial mat
an independent outside auditor should be called in to go over

- 68 -

books if there is any doubt as to their accuracy. Another approach which is used by the police in detective stories, if not in real life, is to ask a person to relate an incident over again at a later date. Carefully compare a tape recording of the first account of the incident with the later telling of it, to see if it has changed substantially. The problem is that we simply accept what people say at face value, when a little checking around might determine the accuracy of their statements.

Keeping a Record of the Facts: A Necessary Evil

The most common reason for inaccuracy in solving problems is actually not deception, but rather a lack of organization or just plain "sloppiness". I mentioned earlier that people's descriptions of the problem situation should be tape recorded. Would you normally go to the trouble of doing that? Probably not. Many people would not even bother to write down what was said, thereby relying fully on their memory of the conversation. When I first read this quote by Dr. Ralph Nichols, author of the definitive book *Are You Listening*, I was startled: He wrote: ". . .immediately after the average person has listened to someone talk, he remembers only about half of what was said, *no matter how carefully he thought he had listened*." If you had only half of the entries in your checkbook right, what chance would you have of arriving at a correct balance? None, right? That's about the same chance you'll have of solving your problems if you don't bother to keep accurate records of the facts involved.

A major obstacle to verifying facts is this one aspect of human nature: *People hate to write things down and keep records*. The chances are that you're no different. When the end of the year comes and we have to face doing our taxes, most of us have to dig back through chaotic piles of receipts and checkstubs. Few of us keep accurate records as we go along, yet there is documented evidence that accurate record-keeping greatly improves people's control over many different aspects of their lives. One outstanding example is in the area of dieting. Doctors attempting to help patients reduce weight often have them write down exactly what they eat every time they consume even the smallest morsel. At the end of the day most people who do this for the first time are astonished at how much incidental food they have consumed. When I was in the Army, I noticed that fat Army cooks seemed to rarely eat a big meal, but they constantly nibbled their way to obesity without even noticing it.

Time management experts similarly have people keep minute-by-minute records of their use of time. First-time users of this technique are amazed at how much time has slipped through their fingers during incidental phone calls, momentary conversations or prolonged searches for missing papers, files, keys, etc. Like keeping a food log or a time log, keeping an *accurate log* of conversations and other facts found during your problem solving investigation, will pay off handsomely when you sit down to tally up everything you have gathered. You may find the solution pops right out at you when you put all of the facts and numbers up on a chart, or when you diagram the exact details of the chain of events that led up to the problem situation.

Beliefs, Assumptions and Other Arbitrary Elements

Arbitrary: *1. Determined by whim or caprice. 2. Based on or subject to individual judgment or discretion.*

Input also includes your own ideas, beliefs, assumptions, knowledge, feelings and attitudes. The chapters on defining your problem were designed to help you clarify these ordinarily *arbitrary* elements. Arbitraries can make the solving of a problem incredibly difficult. When you were in grammar school or high school, or perhaps even college, I'm sure you encountered, as I did, teachers who graded inconsistently and arbitrarily. Depending on their mood, you could get an "A" one day and a "C" the next, on exactly the same paper. Similarly, working in a business under a moody supervisor, you may have found that the same job performance which was acceptable one day, could bring criticisms and complaints the next day. Faced with such arbitrary whims of judgment, finding a consistent solution to a problem could be all but impossible.

When you come to the chapters on *Communication Power* and *Morale Power,* you may find some ideas to help you solve problems presented by other arbitrary people, but for now let's look at some arbitrary elements which are directly under *your* control: your own ideas, beliefs and, most important of all, assumptions and conjectures. I had never realized how thoroughly people confuse assumptions with facts until I heard a talk by a Santa Barbara, California-based consultant named Lawrence T. Winard. Mr. Winard demonstrated how far we have gone in accepting assumptions and conjectures in place of facts, by going through the *front page* of a major Los Angeles newspaper. Theoretically a newspaper prints facts in the lead stories and places opinions in editorial or commentary sections or columns. Mr. Winard proceeded to circle every item of conjecture and every assumption on the front page. It was startling! The page was full of unsupported inferences, assumptions and conjectures. Little wonder critics speak of "trial by the press!"

In the chapter on "Defining Problems," you will recall I asked you to describe a typical problem. I asked you to look for words in your description which indicated how *difficult* the problem was. I then noted that a typical problem described in one of my workshops was "My car is broken down and I *can't* afford to get it fixed." I asked you to notice the word "can't," and the use of it in describing a problem like: "I can't get my kids to do any work around the house." Consider this word "can't" a bit more: At the beginning of Chapter 2, I noted all of the synonyms of *"define"* given in a *Thesaurus*. The second definition of *define* has to do with setting boundaries, as in defining the exact dimensions of a plot of land. Assumptions, like definitions of words and ideas also set boundaries. Some of the synonyms for *define* were *bound, confine, limit*. There is a KEY principle at work here:

The way you define a problem can set definite limitations on your ability to solve it.

The word "can't" is probably the *most* limiting word in the English language, and it implies an underlying *assumption of defeat* as a foregone conclusion. A far less limiting (and more truthful) statement would have been, "I have not yet found a workable strategy to resolve my problem."

In an effort to help people in my workshops break through negative assumptions, I ask them to re-state their problem in a way that suggests the possibility of a solution. You will recall that the fellow with the car in need of repair restated his problem as follows: "My car is broken down and I have not yet accumulated the funds to fix it or found a good mechanic who would fix it for less money." This restatement didn't immediately solve his problem, but it did put it into a more solvable perspective than "I *can't* fix my car." The lady whose kids wouldn't do work around the house restated her problem as follows: "I haven't yet found a way to communicate with my kids that will get them to willingly do work around the house." In each of these cases the new definition of the problem pointed in the direction of looking for new skills, additional resources, or new sources of help and information.

The difference between a conjecture and an assumption is that conjecture is usually *presented* as an opinion or inference. Assumptions are more treacherous because they are generally supposed to be *true*, without evidence or proof. By identifying and challenging your assumptions in a problem situation, you accomplish two things:

1. *You separate the definite facts from the <u>arbitrary</u> elements.*

2. *You open up the possibility of <u>unfixing</u> some mental roadblocks in your problem solving path.*

The best way to get a handle on this matter of separating facts from arbitrary assumptions, beliefs and conjectures, is to apply the technique to solving one of your own problems. The checklist at the end of this chapter asks you to do just that. It is not an easy thing to do. If it was easy to recognize when you are making an assumption not based on fact, you probably would do it less frequently and would have fewer problems as a result. You have to be really tough on yourself and. question *every* assumption and assumed "fact." You need to fully *verify* facts and challenge arbitrary ideas, beliefs, attitudes, feelings, assumptions and conjectures. If you can discipline yourself to do that, you will be well on your way to becoming a "super-solver."

The Power of Effective Input

I hope you now have a better idea of the importance of carrying out the "input" step of the problem-solving sequence with great care and thoroughness. It can be the key to a rapid solution to nearly any problem. Keep this fundamental rule in mind:

> *Increasing relevant knowledge and skill and finding out and verifying pertinent facts and viewpoints should be the first tactic in your overall problem solving strategy.*

Throughout this book, you will be asked to list possible solutions to problems, to consider ways to test those solutions, and to work out specific applications of the solutions. But the effectiveness of your solutions will usually *have already been determined* by how well you have defined the problem, gathered and checked all of the facts, and considered all of the possible solutions and their consequences *before* taking action.

PROBLEM SOLVING POWER
CHECKLIST NUMBER SIX

Fact: *1. Something known with certainty. 3. Something that has been objectively verified. 4. Something having real, demonstrable existence.*

Conjecture: *1. Inference based on inconclusive or incomplete evidence; guesswork. 2. An opinion or conclusion based on inference.*

Assumption: *2. A statement accepted or supposed true without proof or demonstration.*

— Familiarize —

1. Write down a new statement of your problem (notice that you describe it a bit differently every time you write it down).

2. Write down three facts — that is, three things you know for *certain* — about the problem situation.

3. After each fact, write down *how you learned* that it was a fact. Note if someone told you, or if your read it somewhere. For each fact, write down the *source* of that fact, and ask yourself how reliable you would consider that information source.

4. Write down three things you have believed or *assumed* about the problem situation, but do not know for certain.

5. Take one of the assumptions you have just written and think of someone else who has based an action on a similar assumption. What happened? Did his or her assumption prove to be correct? If your assumption is wrong, what might happen?

6. Take the second of your assumptions: Did you make that assumption in an earlier problem situation? Review that previous problem. What happened? Did the assumption prove to be correct?

7. Now look at your third assumption. What evidence do you have that it is correct? If it is true, what action are you likely to take, based on that assumption? If not true, what then?

8. Now take each of your assumptions and write down the exact opposite assumption. For example if you assume you won't get a job you're applying for, assume that you *will*, or if you don't have enough money to carry out a project, assume that you have *too much* money to bother doing it. Get the idea? Tell what would happen for each one. Then do this for any other assumptions you're making about your problem situation.

9. How would your behavior change if the opposite assumptions you just wrote down were true? How would your problem change?

10. Now do a thorough *inventory* of facts and arbitrary ideas, opinions, beliefs, viewpoints and assumptions:

a. Get *everyone* involved in the problem situation to tell you what they perceive the problem to be and what they believe should be done to solve it.

b. Find out what other information is needed to resolve the problem. Then find out where that knowledge might be obtained or who might help you find it.

c. Look in trade magazines, specialized reference books, and the periodical review of magazines and publications to learn what people with similar problems have done to solve them.

d. Talk to rivals, competitors, or people in a similar business or situation. Find out *directly* if they have had a similar problem and, if so, how they solved it.

e. For business problems: survey suppliers, employees, contract services, customers and perhaps even prospective customers. Ask for their reactions to the problem and solutions you might want to try. "Solutions" which offend people on whom you depend for survival could create bigger problems rather than the intended solution.

f. Check with city, state or even federal authorities to find out if there are any restrictions you have to consider when formulating a solution. You may have to go to the extreme of doing an environmental impact study.

g. Gather information on the physical and mental stability of people who may be affected by possible solutions to the problem. Solutions which make people angry, uncomfortable or sick will only create larger problems. Often it's necessary to do a kind of "human impact study" before deciding on and implementing a solution.

h. Take a piece of notebook paper and draw a vertical line down the middle. Head the left column "Facts" and the right column "Arbitraries and Assumptions." Then write back and forth between the columns as you list either facts, arbitaries or assumptions, but be very sure to include only facts of which you are *certain* in the left column. Make separate notes of ways to check the accuracy of your facts as you go along.

i. If you think of a new solution approach, add it to your *Power Solutions* list at the back of this book.

Making erroneous assumptions can lead to
serious problems and great anguish.

As a result of a thoughtful appraisal of a problem,
an intuitive solution will often appear.

7. BE WILLING TO JUST KNOW

"All that is is the result of what we have thought."
The Suttapitka
From the Theravada Buddhist Scriptures

When I was a kid in high school in the '50s, it seemed I had endless problems. From what I've been able to see, most adolescents feel that way, but I came from a broken family, I lived with a grandmother and an aunt, and I worked at seven different odd jobs simultaneously to contribute to my own support. Compared to kids around me, it seemed I had more problems than most of them.

Jack, my closest friend, was exactly the opposite. His family owned the local restaurant in the small town where we lived, and he seemed to have everything he wanted and more. He had something else which gave him an enormous advantage. He was incredibly *lucky*! When the local theatre started a weekly bingo game to attract people from neighboring towns, Jack won the largest prize available on the opening day. And he proceeded to win time after time until they barred him from playing. This was how Jack lived his life. It seemed that whenever he encountered a problem situation, he intuitively went in a direction where a solution was just waiting for him. To me it looked like a mystical power. I think many people would have said he had some special psychic ability.

There can be little doubt that some people are luckier than others and that some people have more problems than others. Insurance companies are well aware of the fact that some people are "accident prone," therefore the companies structure their rates so that people who have more accidents pay more. If some people are "accident prone" or "bad luck prone" then it should not be surprising that someone like my friend Jack would be "good luck prone" and thus tend to be more problem free. Max Gunther, the author of *The Luck Factor*, the best popular book on luck that I have read, says that good luck is no accident. For more than twenty years he collected the stories of hundreds of exceptionally lucky and *markedly unlucky* people. In his book he relates the fact that lucky people are different. They share five traits, or patterns of behavior, which constitute what he calls *The Luck Factor*. If his research is accurate, the cultivating of these patterns of behavior could greatly improve a person's ability to solve problems, to avoid problems, and to live a more problem-free existence.

I've included this luck factor because it is often possible to solve a problem instantly by drawing on what Max Gunther calls "the hunching skill". It is that intuitive "sixth sense" which often steers people like my friend Jack in the direction of the best possible solution to a problem. In the last twenty years research on the brain has enabled scientists to establish a difference between how the left brain and the right brain function. People who are mainly left-brain oriented are very analytical and methodical. People who are right-brain oriented are more intuitive. Max Gunther tells about Conrad Hilton, who he says made his millions partly due to a hunching skill so "finely tuned that at times it seemed occult." What he means by this is that lucky people stay very in tune with their intuitive sense. They know that not all hunches can be trusted, but by *tuning in* and *testing* their hunches, more and more they can learn which hunches to act on and which not to.

When I was discharged from the U.S. Army in 1961, I went through a special training program which was designed to increase I.Q., alertness and reaction time. Hundreds of test scores showing increases of twenty points or more were presented to the Department of the Navy as evidence of the program's effectiveness. As a result of that training program I experienced a thirty point increase in I.Q. To test the increase I took the tests offered by MENSA, the high I.Q. society, which requires an I.Q. in the upper 2% of the population for membership. Only a couple of years earlier I had been thoroughly tested by the U.S. Army and had been rated at 123 I.Q. on what was the standard test score range at that time. I was more than 20 points below the score required for MENSA membership. After I took the training, the MENSA tests revealed that I had indeed jumped to 153 or better.

What had brought about this major change in demonstrable intelligence? The main emphasis of the training was on *maintaining a steady focus of attention* and, above all, observing accurately. The training enabled me to greatly overcome any tendency to be distracted and to focus much more quickly, whether inwardly on the answer to a question, or outwardly on what another person was saying to me. This ability to *fine-tune my inward focus* brought along with it an increased ability to *tune into intuitive hunches*. For example, the house that I now live in was purchased as a result of a hunch that the "sold" sign on it was not accurate and that it was actually still available for purchase. Upon closer investigation my wife and I learned that the realtor himself was attempting to buy the house, which was up for a probate sale bid, at a very low bid. It appeared that he had placed the "sold" sign on the house to discourage other bidders. Because of that hunch we were able to obtain the house for at least fifteen percent less than the going rate for a similar house.

Judgment, Intuition and Decisions

In the last chapter I emphasized the importance of putting facts ahead of assumptions. Quite a few years ago Peter Drucker, the great guru of all business consultants, wrote in an article on decision-making:

> Most of the earlier books on problem-solving or decision-making went into details about finding the facts. Many businessmen pride themselves that they always base their decisions on facts. Our modern study of decision-making leads us to take a dim view of this assertion.
>
> Actually we must always base our decision on assumptions regarding the future; and the only facts we can ever have are in respect to the past . . . . What we need is to define the expectations for the future that govern our decisions.

Dr. Drucker says that he has yet to sit in on a meeting where there is not a flood of figures and "facts," but often the facts are *not relevant.* The expectations have not been thought out exactly and so it was never clear *what facts were needed!* Max Gunther writing in his chapter on "The Hunching Skill," says: *"When a hunch comes, always ask yourself whether the underlying facts could be there. Ask whether you could have absorbed data about the situation."*

He sets down several rules and corollaries for trusting and not trusting hunches:

1. *Learn to assess the data base.*
2. *Never trust a hunch about somebody you have just met.*
3. *Never fall back on hunching to avoid work.*
4. *Never confuse a hunch with a hope.*
5. *Make room for hunches to grow.*
6. *Don't smother a hunch by "figuring out."*
7. *Collect "soft" facts along with the hard.*

Regarding this last rule, Max stresses that "Hunches are made of facts, but they come as feelings." He says, "To hunch soundly you must *listen to your feelings,* respect them, give them a full hearing." Another specialist who provides a way for you to amplify your "hunching skill" is Eugene Gendlin, author of a book entitled *Focusing.* He says that a feeling about a situation always contains more than could have been figured out intellectually. To accentuate this ability he has you make contact with a large, vague, generalized feeling and then focus on smaller and smaller parts of that feeling until a useful realization occurs.

Some people make better contact with their intuitive power while writing. Others do better meditating or reflecting. I have always preferred writing. My favorite guide on this subject is Dr. Ira Progoff, author of *At a Journal Workshop*, and *The Practice of Process Meditation*. Dr. Progoff provides a *dialogue* approach to tapping one's intuitive awareness. Through his "Intensive Journal" method, he guides each student into a series of written dialogues with many dimensions of life. He calls one of the accompanying processes, "Twilight Imagery," which he describes as follows:

> *The key to twilight imaging lies in the fact that it takes place in the twilight state between waking and sleeping. We find that by working actively in that intermediate state of consciousness, we are able to reach depths of ourselves with which it is very difficult to make contact by any other means. . . . We turn our attention inward and we wait in stillness, and let ourselves observe the various forms of imagery that present themselves . . . . Then, at various convenient points in the process, we gather our observations and our beholdings together and we record them in our Twilight Imagery Log.*

As you can see, there are many ways to approach getting in touch with the intuitive level of your consciousness. Regardless of which you choose, to accomplish any effective problem solving using these techniques, you must approach them as a *discipline*. Otherwise simply chasing hunches and feelings could lead you on many a wild goose chase.

Peter Drucker adds another word of caution about the pitfalls of confusing approaches to making decisions. He says people,

> ". . . *do not organize their decision-making. They tend to do by intuition, those parts of the process that can best be done rationally, and tend to be rational and fact-based in those parts that should be matters of judgement.*"

As you work through the checklists in this book, it is my hope that you will increase both sides of your problem solving ability: That you will gain an ability to recognize and separate facts from assumptions and arbitrary opinion, but that you will also become more able to *tune into* your own intuitive awareness and be more *willing to just know* what is the best course of action to take to resolve a problem.

PROBLEM SOLVING POWER

CHECKLIST NUMBER SEVEN

CHECK YOUR INTUITIVE POWER (Familiarize):

1 - A good beginning approach to solving any problem is to ask yourself: "What do I intuitively sense is the right way to handle this problem?" Write down your hunch about what you should do.

2 - Make a list of all of the people (including groups) involved in your problem situation. Leave space after each list entry to make additional notes about that person or group.

3 - Along side of each entry, write down what you intuitively feel is that person's intent toward you and your problem. Does that person *strongly* hope you will solve your problem? Is the person mildly interested in having you solve your problem? Is the person indifferent to whether you solve the problem or not? Does the person actually intend for you to *not* solve your problem? In each instance, is there any way in which you would change your behavior if your hunch about each of these individuals or groups was true?

4 - Sometimes what seems like an "intuitive" feeling is actually an emotional resistance to facing a part of a problem. Look back at the intuitive feelings you have noted in step one. Do any of your feelings conflict with the *facts* you noted on the previous checklist? What might you do to separate your intuitive hunches from emotional resistances?

5 - Is there some action that you feel is important to take that you have postponed or delayed? If so, why? Think of someone who has not acted when he or she should have because of a feeling of emotional resistance. What happened? Could that person have gotten someone else to help get the job done? Could someone help you overcome any emotional resistance you may have to accomplishing the desired action?

6 - Recall a time when you had a successful hunch. What activities of yours led up to that experience? Is there some way you could reinforce that skill? Is there any similar element in your present problem? Could you draw on past "hunching" successes to help you now? What do you now intuitively feel you should do about your problem?

*Communication power requires the courage
to reach out and express oneself fully.*

8. COMMUNICATION POWER

*Speech is civilization itself. The word, even the most
contradictory word, preserves contact. It is silence
which isolates.*
        —Thomas Mann

 Many problems are simply the result of communication misunderstandings. These situations arise when people fail to give their full attention to a communication. What situation annoys you most where people don't give you their full attention when you're speaking to them? Is it the waiter or waitress who doesn't get your order right? Or is it the clerk who misunderstands your request and brings you the wrong merchandise? Or a spouse or fellow worker who says "O.K." when you ask for something but never brings it as though you had never spoken?

 Many of the upsets and disturbances we encounter in life, occur because of misunderstood communication. Each of these upsets can rob us of a little bit of the attention we would otherwise have free to focus on perceiving and enjoying life. A communication is often misunderstood because the listener did not really *grasp*—perceive or comprehend—what was said. You can see from the dictionary definition of *comprehend* and *perceive* that fewer misunderstandings would occur if people really had mastered these skills:

"comprehend" (tr.v.) 1. To grasp mentally; understand or know. 2. To take in, include or embrace.

"perceive" (tr.v.) 1. To become aware of directly, through any of the senses; especially to see or hear. 2. To take notice of; observe; detect. 3. To become aware of in one's mind; achieve understanding of; apprehend; grasp.

 Communication is a two-way activity. In conversation you either speak or listen. In computer terminology there is either *input* or *output*. But when real human communication occurs, there is a third element, *comprehension,* which relies much more on the control of attention than on either receiving or sending communication. After all, one can listen mechanically, hearing most of what is said without "paying much attention" to the speaker. And one can speak out of habit, more or less automatically, without thinking about what one is saying. Someone says "How are you" and you reply "Fine" or "O.K." without much thought. Afterwards you may not even recall having spoken to that person. To really receive and comprehend what a speaker is saying, you would need to cultivate a greater *determination* to listen closely and to grasp exactly what the other person is *intending* for you to receive.

When you are in the process of collecting information to solve a problem, it is *crucial* that you get your facts straight! As I mentioned before, when you're adding up a column of numbers and one of the numbers in the column is wrong, you know the answer will be wrong as well. The same is true of solving business and life problems. If the facts are not correct, they won't add up to a correct solution. When your attention is not focused on someone you're listening to, you are likely to miss some of what is said. For an effective communication connection to occur, both the speaker and listener must have their attention fully focused in the present.

Self-to-Self Communication

There is another connection which demands even more that attention be focused in the present. That is the connection *within yourself*, between the physical perceptions of seeing or hearing, and the registering of what was seen or heard within your understanding. You could diagram the action as follows:

SPEAKER'S WORDS HEARD→WORDS UNDERSTOOD→IDEA GRASPED
(Input) → *(Inner Connection)* → *(Comprehension)*

There are several pitfalls along this pathway which can prevent the idea sent by the original speaker from really being comprehended by the listener: (1) The words might not be spoken clearly or heard clearly. (2) The listener may not have an accurate or agreed upon definition for all of the words, and thus may not understand what the speaker really meant. (3) Finally the listener might not really have his "mind in gear", that is, he or she may not be fully *connected* inside. Attention may not be completely focused on what is going on. When this happens the conversation will be forgotten in minutes or even seconds. Dr. Ralph Nichols, author of *Are You Listening*, says, "Extensive tests have led to this general conclusion: immediately after the average person has listened to someone talk, he remembers only about half of what he heard, no matter how carefully he thought he had listened."

EXERCISE

There are several simple exercises you can practice to improve your listening effectiveness:

1.   If you don't clearly hear or understand what a person says, ask him or her to repeat it. Most people will be flattered that you care enough about what they have to say to really want to understand it.

2. *If you read or hear a word you don't have a definition for, ask for a definition or write the word down and look it up in a dictionary as soon as you have a chance. Then practice using it until you're comfortable with it.*

3. *Whenever in doubt, repeat back what you think a person said to find out if you understood it correctly.*

4. *Constantly practice asking, listening and checking for understanding to improve your listening and comprehension abilities.*

Comprehension and Confusion

Problem: *A question or situation that presents uncertainty, perplexity or difficulty.*

Perplex: *To confuse or puzzle; bewilder.*
                        The American Heritage Dictionary

Recall the last time you were caught in a traffic jam because of an accident and couldn't move your car an inch. Did you have a feeling of utter futility? Did you feel your space was completely restricted? What effect did the experience have on your attention? Were you able to separate your mind from the confusion of the moment and think creatively and constructively about other things while you waited? Many people could not.

Sociologists have written lengthy texts about Man's instinct for defending his territory against invasion. Invasion of one's space is usually perceived on some level as a threat to survival. Whenever there is a threat to survival, your full attention automatically focuses on that threat. A similar phenomenon occurs when there is great turmoil or confusion. Instinctively you tend to interpret this chaotic condition as a threat to survival. Have you noticed how other drivers react to an accident, often creating a traffic jam? Confusion usually triggers intense emotions in people, especially if they feel threatened by it.

There is a natural tendency, when faced with a confusing situation, to seek out a safe or stable place to get out of the confusion. Physically this could be looking for shelter in a storm or a place to get out of the way of a mob. Mentally it could be looking for *a safe idea* to get away from a mental confusion. When people break up a love affair they often feel confused. They may go home to their parents to have a stable, safe, quiet place where they can "gather themselves together," or they may foolishly grab the first new person who comes along to fill the empty void and alleviate the uncertainty created by losing their loved one.

There is a similar tendency to retreat after a new effort to reach out and expand fails. A common example is the failed entrepreneur. I have known several people who put their life savings into a new small business which didn't work out. When the business failed they became very confused and went back to the safest job they had had previously in which they had felt "safe," regardless of how much of a drop in income that retreat meant.

What does this have to do with problems and confusion? Apparently there is a natural inclination for people to *retreat* from the unknown and the uncomprehendable. Perhaps it traces back in the group psyche of Mankind to a prehistoric instinct for the survival of the species. Whatever the source of the phenomenon may be, there is a tendency for a *problem to be created* whenever a communication occurs which is "over the head" of the recipient. In general people feel threatened by communication they can't comprehend.

Recall a time a teacher, boss, sergeant or other person in authority gave you an instruction you didn't understand, and also didn't give you a chance to ask for clarification. Recall how helpless you felt when you couldn't do what you were supposed to because you didn't understand how. What do most people do when faced with a confusion of this sort? A wise person admits to not understanding and continues to press for clarification. Unfortunately some people revert to childhood solutions and fake a disability or illness to get sympathy. I saw this happen on numerous occasions when I was in the army. Some guys actually became physically ill (or psychosomatically ill). Of course there were those who bluffed their way through and pretended to understand. This is a common reaction to a failure to comprehend.

There is only one workable solution to this kind of situation. It is always best to confront your lack of comprehension and *to communicate until it gets cleared up.* The KEY to solving a comprehension problem is to realize:

> *You can only resolve a comprehension confusion by facing your failure to grasp the communication situation and by continuing to communicate until you understand it fully.*

Denial and Distortion

Dr. Carl Rogers, the developer of *Client-Centered Therapy* in the 1950's, wrote about "Barriers and Gateways to Communication". He discussed two practices of people which prevent them from really understanding others. One practice he called *denial*, and the other, *distortion*.

Denial occurs when a person hears something he or she *doesn't really want to hear* and so shuts it out altogether. A parent who is told that a son or daughter has become addicted to drugs often reacts in this manner. *Distortion* occurs when a person doesn't want to hear *all of what is said* and so mentally *changes part of it* to fit what he or she chooses to believe. Distortion occurs so commonly, you may seldom ever notice it.

Try this experiment. Get a friend to agree to try to literally copy everything you say. Start with a short sentence. Have your friend try to repeat it back to you exactly. Then try longer and longer sentences. Have him or her repeat each sentence until it has been copied perfectly. Notice the tendency to leave out words or to change them, even with only a few words. Then have your friend deliver a sentence to you, and you try to make an exact copy yourself. Build up longer and longer sentences. Repeat each one until it has been copied perfectly. Notice that you are both able to focus attention far better when you strive to make *exact* copies.

When you insist on *completely* understanding any communication which comes your way, and you make certain others have *really understood* what you have said, you will find there is far less confusion in your life. When there is less confusion, you will also find your attention is freer to focus on the things in life that give you the greatest pleasure, rather than the problems which are generated by confusions and misunderstandings. That greater freedom of attention focus will, in turn, make it easier to listen to what people say and to comprehend what they mean. It can lead to a continual upward spiral of greater ability, greater clarity and greater satisfaction with living.

How Faulty Communicators Create Problems

One of the definitions of "a problem," is: "*A person who is difficult to deal with.*" Look back over your life and think of someone you considered to be "a problem person." My guess is that, if you analyzed how that person communicated, you would find he or she had one or more of the following communication problems:

- *Compulsive outflow — talks constantly.*
- *Inhibited outflow — shy; hardly speaks.*
- *Compulsive inflow — can't say no; accepts anything.*
- *Inhibited inflow — won't listen.*

The *compulsive outflow* communicator may be the most difficult to tolerate. This person communicates endlessly without ever "shutting up," and usually has an *inhibited inflow* problem as well. He or she thus will be incapable of listening to you for more than a few moments before interrupting you and continuing to talk. I'm certain you've encountered a person like this somewhere along the way, and probably more than one.

The *inhibited outflow* person is usually painfully shy. Because this kind of person waits a very long time to express grievances or communicate the fact that there is a problem, circumstances may reach crisis proportions before you realize that something is wrong and must be handled. A child who doesn't tell his or her parents about pains or discomforts early on, may become critically ill before the need for treatment is discovered. Employees who fail to communicate to their employer about problems in the workplace, may unexpectedly quit. A similarly inhibited spouse may refrain from telling a marital partner about intolerable habits or living circumstances and then suddenly leave one day. People with this type of communication problem usually expect an employer, spouse or other associate to simply *notice* the condition without being told. When the condition is not noticed and corrected, they may suddenly explode and leave.

The *compulsive inflow* type is the person who "can't say no." This individual accepts orders, demands for help, pan-handlers, criticisms, endless suggestions and often even physical abuse without taking a firm stand and refusing to tolerate it. This behavior may be perceived from the outside as that of a perpetual "victim." Courses in "assertiveness training," often based on Manuel Smith's famous book, *When I Say No I Feel Guilty,* can now be found in most university extension programs and adult eduction programs. They can help correct the condition.

The common denominator in the behavior of people with severe communication problems, is an *inability to accurately perceive* what is going on with the other guy and to achieve a balanced response. The compulsive outflow person never seems to notice that others have *tuned out* his or her communication long ago. The inhibited inflow person has failed to perceive the value in listening to what others have to say. The inhibited outflow person has failed to perceive the fact that his or her communication and viewpoint may not only be welcome, but may also be valuable to those around him or her. The compulsive inflow person has failed to realize that saying no when it is appropriate benefits both self and everyone else involved.

All of these communication liabilities create and/or perpetuate problems. Rational, effective communication requires honesty and an approximate balance of inflow and outflow between communicating parties. Otherwise communication problems will develop.

How Not to Get Others to Change

The effort to deal with "problem persons" begins in childhood. The usual method parents use to try to change their children's problem behavior is to: (1) *tell them what they're doing wrong,* and (2) *tell them how to do it right.* Thomas Harris, in his famous psychological text *I'm O.K., You're O.K.,* identified the roles of "parent," "child," and "adult" as the three main approaches to interacting with others. Unfortunately the compulsive "parent" approach is the one most used by authoritarian teachers, bosses, spouses, friends and family members of every age. In an early chapter I introduced you to the vital concept of separating facts from assumptions. The two most erroneous assumptions, made by the compulsive parent-type trying to change the behavior of a problem person, are:

1. *Assuming the solution which is best for oneself is also best for someone else.* and
2. *Assuming that telling another what is best will get him or her to change or to solve a problem.*

Since you've lived enough years to be interested in reading a book like this one, I have to assume you've tried suggesting solutions to your friend's or some family member's problems. I would guess that you've discovered that such suggestions are seldom if ever accepted and applied. It seems that solutions are like houses and cars: If they're borrowed or rented they're never treated like ones that are owned. People only totally value that which is their own. The trick to getting a problem person to apply your solution, therefore, is to get that person to believe *the solution is his or her own!*

Using Questions to Change Problem Behavior

Around 400 B.C., the Greek philosopher Socrates began to demonstrate the process of arriving at truth through argument. In the dialogues of his pupil Plato, he is portrayed as using questions to gradually lead an opponent, with an opposing point of view, to change his mind and finally accept his point of view. Socrates accomplishes this feat by finding small points of agreement and using them to lead to larger points of agreement which eventually contradict his opponent's original position. With diligent practice, you find you can achieve a similar result with clever questioning.

In Chapter Five, on *Morale Power,* I introduced you to some of the ideas of my friend Ed Morler, who conducts negotiating skill seminars for major financial institutions. One of Ed's favorite tools to teach negotiating power is an exercise he calls "probing." He points out that in the process of negotiation, it is a common practice for your opponent to attempt to manipulate you by making an *outrageous* statement or demand. The purpose of this practice is to temporarily shock you, to throw you off-stride, to *introvert* your attention and make you more vulnerable. Ed says that when this happens, a negotiator is most prone to give in and make a concession. The way to avoid making a concession is to *respond with a request for more information!* Ask questions! Ed calls this "probing." His idea is that many conflicts can be resolved when the real needs and desires of both parties are fully understood. He says you should always try for a win-win situation rather than a win-lose situation. In his "probing" exercise, the student negotiator practices asking questions to learn as much as possible about an opponent's viewpoint on a particular subject.

In the next few pages of this chapter, I will introduce you to Don Holmes, a consultant who makes a living by solving problems. He solves the problems simply by asking questions in carefully structured interviews. The basis of his questioning is the assumption that the individuals who are part of a problem situation, potentially have the solutions if asked the right questions. I suggest that the solution to your problem of how to deal with a problem person may be to *ask more questions.* Learn as much as you can about the person, preferably by asking the person directly. If you can't get direct answers, it may be necessary to learn what you need to know from family, friends or fellow-workers. Most behavior is shaped by past experiences and relationships. Find out what shaped this problem person. It will help you handle him or her in a far more effective way.

There are a few rules you must follow when asking questions. If you fail to follow these rules, you may make the situation worse rather than better. Practice following these rules by questioning people who are *easy to deal with first.* When you feel you have mastered the art of questioning, while sticking to these rules, *then* try questioning a difficult person. As a general principle always give yourself wins rather than losses. This principle alone will tend to make you more of a *Super Solver!*

— RULES FOR EFFECTIVE QUESTIONING —

1. *Know in advance exactly what questions you want answered. Don't wait until you are actually in the conversation to construct the questions. If possible, practice them out loud*

first, or at least write the questions down. Notice how slight changes in wording can alter the meaning of the questions. You don't want your question misunderstood. If it is not worded correctly, you will get an answer to a question you didn't intend to ask.

2. Ask only one question at a time. Repeat it or vary it if you do not get an answer right away. Do not ask a second question until you have gotten an answer to the first question, except for asking for a clarification on any answer you don't understand. If one question inescapably leads to a second question, get it answered and then come back to your first question. Never leave a question unanswered if at all possible.

3. Even though a person avoids your question, answers a different question or changes the subject, keep coming back to that question in one form or another until you get an answer to the question.

4. Be _totally attentive_ while asking questions and listening to conversation or answers to your questions. Look directly at the person's face and eyes. Do not let your eyes or your mind wander. Your attention won't wander if you are _actively participating_ in the conversation. If something distracts you and you miss what has been said, ask for a repeat or clarification, but do so without interrupting.

5. The general rule is to never interrupt a person's train of thought once you have asked a question and are listening for the answer. Some people, however, seem to talk on and on without taking a moment's pause. There is an art to _constructively interrupting_ to redirect a person back to answering your question or to clarifying a specific point. Watch for the end of a sentence where the person must take a breath. Then jump in quickly with your question or redirecting statement. To add emphasis to your question or statement, you must sometimes get the person's attention by suddenly standing up, sitting down, shifting body position, speaking more loudly, gesturing, or otherwise making a body motion which is not offensive.

6. When you get an answer to a question, express your appreciation for the information. Acknowledge the individual for being willing to open up and take you into his or her confidence and to share this information.

Communication as the Link to Solutions

Several years ago a business opportunities salesman named Don Holmes made an observation which changed his life. As he went about his task of locating businesses for sale and looking for possible buyers of those businesses, he noted that many business owners didn't put their business up for sale until it was in trouble to such a degree that it wasn't a good buy for anyone. They would then, of course, want an extraordinary price for the business based on the days when it had been doing well. Naturally Don found such businesses almost impossible to sell unless he could get the owner to lower the price, or to invest some time and money to bring the business back up to a level of performance where it could be sold.

After appraising business after business, Don came to realize that most of the businesses that were failing were failing because of a lack of *communication*. He also realized that he could probably fill that communication need and thereby raise a business to a level where it could be sold. He decided to test out his hypothesis. He approached a prospective client company and asked for a list of current problems. He then quoted a price and guaranteed to resolve all of those problems (within a reasonable time) or they would pay nothing.

He obtained the agreement of management to allow him to interview every employee in the company, including management, to obtain ideas of possible solutions to the problems. He also promised that all interview responses would be kept anonymous so no one would be penalized for critical responses. Because he (the consultant) would be doing the interviewing, and because he would promise to keep all answers anonymous, he could be certain of obtaining frank, honest answers to all questions. This was something management could never be certain of accomplishing if they conducted the interviews.

He got management to agree to implement all solutions to problems which were obvious solutions based on a concensus of answers from various employees interviews. If they chose not to implement a solution, they would waive the guarantee of results and their right to withhold payment from the consultant.

The Result: Within three to six months, in not only the test business, but in subsequent clients companies as well, the answers and observations of the employees provided probable solutions to every major problem which had been specified at the start of the consultation. It became obvious that people within the companies knew, but withheld, the vital information needed to resolve the problems. There were many different reasons, but all were nullified by the interviewing technique of the consultant.

Generalizing the Result to Solve Other Problems

I, and some fellow consultants, were very impressed with the results of this approach to resolving business problems, but we questioned whether it would be generally applicable under all circumstances. We felt the system had been completely successful only because it had been tried in so few companies and most of them were fairly small companies. We looked for an underlying principle behind the success of the system to see if it could be expanded to include any business or company, regardless of size. If the system worked with a company, it would also be reasonable to expect that it might work within any group, whether social, commercial or political. Even an *individual's* problems usually occur within the context of some interpersonal or group activity. Solutions which work for a group on a large scale should also work for an individual on a smaller scale.

Put simply, Holmes' idea was that any business or organization is a closed system. If a problem occurs within the system, the solution should also be found within the system. The word *organization* is based on the same root as the word *organism*. There are many parallels between how a business organization and a human organism operate. Both are clearly defined, self-contained entities. The KEY concept is therefore that:

> *If any of the organs or perceptions of a body are put out of communication with the body as a whole, the survival of the entire body is put at risk.*

Through his interviewing process, acting as an intermediary, Don Holmes performed the equivalent of putting the hands, eyes, ears, lungs and other organs back in touch with the brain. Looked at from this point of view, it's not surprising that these companies became able to recover from their sick condition once effective communication was reestablished!

Addressing the Total Organization

In our evaluation of Don Holmes' consulting procedure, we found one major flaw. The procedure assumed that the physical plant of the company, with its employees and management, comprised the entire "closed system". In actuality the "closed system" of a business includes *all* of the sources of *incoming and outgoing* communications involved with that business enterprise, as well as all of the sources of *internal* communications. These can include:

- *Customers*
- *Suppliers*
- *Creative service providers*
- *Trade publications & other information sources*
- *Morale & recreation development terminals*
- *Trade & ethical standards associations*
- *Advertising & promotional media contacts*
- *Outside sales reps.*
- *Trade unions, outside contractors & job shops*
- *Distribution houses, trade show and other expansion contacts*
- *Business associates, partners, investors, members of the board, etc.*
- *Competitors*
- *Family & friends*

You can see that with this complete list, you will *now* have total input from all of the related *incoming, internal and outgoing* elements involved in this business's (not-so-closed) system. With this modification to the consulting procedure, which would include interviewing *all* of these entities, you might actually be secure in advertising:

YOUR BUSINESS PROBLEM FULLY SOLVED OR YOU
PAY NOTHING. CALL FOR FREE APPRAISAL.

There would, of course, be some restrictions. When a prospective client calls, it would be vital to ask the following questions during the appraisal. These same questions would apply when evaluating any business problem:

1. How long have you been in business?
2. What is the most important problem you wish to handle?
3. When was your business last running perfectly well with no trace of that problem?
4. When did you notice the first indication that this problem existed?
5. To what did you first attribute those indications?
6. When was the scope of the problem fully recognized?
7. What efforts have been made to correct this problem? When were they first begun?
8. What efforts were at least partially successful? Which ones failed

totally?

9. Do you really believe the problem can be solved?

10. How would you know if a corrective measure was really working?

11. Would anyone benefit from the problem never being solved?

12. What result would tell you that this specific problem is now fully (or will be fully) solved?

After this appraisal you would have a good basis on which to accept or reject the opportunity to solve the problem. To make such an extraordinary claim, you would have to develop *extraordinary* interviewing and communication skills! Most likely you are not acting as a consultant but rather as a principal seeking to solve the problems of your own "closed system", whether it be a company, a family or an individual life. It will only be necessary, therefore, for you to master the degree of communication skill needed to resolve your own set of problems.

Using Communication to Resolve Problems

Unlike many consultants, Don Holmes didn't simply present management with a list of changes to be made based on the information from his interviews. He understood that any management which had become so out of touch with a company that it had failed to solicit solutions to major problems from within the company, would also have difficulty *communicating what needed to be done* to solve the problems to the appropriate staff and employees. Usually he stayed on as a consultant to assist in communications until the suggested solutions were implemented and the problem situations had been resolved.

The KEY to getting this kind of communication solution implemented is to follow through and see that new policies are adopted which will prevent the recurrence of the problem situations. Foremost among these is *a policy to keep people informed!* Once again the *organism* comparison comes into play. If your eye sees your hand about to touch a hot stove and does not send a message to your hand to move it out of the way, it'll get burned. This is so obviously true, it sounds stupidly simple. Nevertheless many companies have such poor internal communications that upper management does not keep the management and personnel of various divisions and departments supplied with critical information.

It is not uncommon to find upper management cautiously doling out information only on a "need to know" basis. Naturally confidential information which should be reserved for staff with a security clearance should not become common knowledge, but in general *the withholding of information creates problems.* Remember, the simplest arithmetic problem cannot be solved unless all of the numbers to be added, subtracted or divided are known. In solving real life problems, the only way to obtain information is through communication. And the only way to avoid having problems occur unnecessarily around you is to *provide* information.

Most problems can be solved, or at least lessened, by communicating more. Ask more questions, listen more intently, and keep others better informed. Many apparent problems may magically vanish.

Three Fundamental Questions:

• *What undelivered communication may be contributing to the persistence of your problem?*

• *What information could you pass on to enable others to do that which could reduce the intensity of your problem situation?*

• *Who could you include in the group to whom you communicate regularly who would be a valuable source of information, inspiration and strength?*

PROBLEM SOLVING POWER

<u>C H E C K L I S T   N U M B E R   E I G H T</u>

— Energize —

CHECK YOUR COMMUNICATION POWER:

1 - Who could you talk to about your problem in terms of what you want or need? Where could you communicate what this problem is preventing you from being? From doing? From obtaining?

2 - Who could you talk to about the *obstacles* standing in the way of you being what you wish to be? Doing what you wish to do? Obtaining what you wish to acquire?

3 - Who could you talk to about scarcities that seem to be causing your problem? Or about resources you are lacking that would enable you to overcome your obstacles and reach your objectives?

4 - Who could you communicate with to increase your creativity in solving problems? What could someone say that would inspire a new invention, design, presentation, activity, connection, market, or creative idea?

5 - Who could you communicate with to increase the knowledge you need to solve your problem? What knowledge, information or skill, that you do not currently possess, could you acquire by communicating more?

6 - Who could you talk to to improve your personal morale and motivation in regard to your problem? Is there something someone could say which would motivate you so strongly that you could resolve your problem despite pessimistic attitudes or negative emotions?

7 – What person or group would be helped if you solved this problem? Have you communicated this fact to that person or group? Is there some person or group who would be harmed if you solved this problem? If so, have you communicated that fact? Is there some person or group who could help you solve it? Have you let that person or group know they could help you solve it?

8 – Is your problem continuing on because of your unwillingness to communicate something to some person or group? If you could communicate anything to anyone with no consequences, what could you communicate which would begin to resolve your problem?

9 – Who could you talk to about speeding up completing those actions which would resolve your problem? Who could you talk to about increasing the amount of time you have to try various solutions to your problem?

10 -Who could you talk to about obstacles in the path of your growth and development toward your larger objectives in life? What could someone say that would increase your expansion into new spaces, new environments, new marketplaces or new activities?

Designing an effective solution is a major art form.

*Creativity power is the result of a willingness
to look for new ways to do things.*

9. CREATIVITY POWER

Some men see things as they are and say "why?"
I dream of things that never were and say "why not?"
George Bernard Shaw—1856-1950

A couple of years ago, I read a comment on an obituary published at the time. The deceased was Sylvan Goldman who passed away in Oklahoma City, Oklahoma, after a very productive 86 years of living. Few of us have ever heard of Sylvan Goldman, but it is likely that every single week of your life, you benefit from one of his inventions. In 1937, Goldman, then a grocery store owner, was looking for a solution to his problem of slow sales and an unwieldy check-out system. The idea he came up with has eternally altered grocery store shopping in America (and probably much of the world by now). He invented the shopping cart. Later he also invented the luggage cart used at airports and bus and train stations around the world. When he died, Sylvan Goldman was worth *two hundred million dollars!*

Actually Goldman didn't really invent anything new. Wire baskets and wheels had been around for a very long time. He just thought of putting them together in a way that no one had imagined before. In reality, few of us know the origin of many of the devices we take for granted today. Another device which you probably use everyday was invented in 1893, by Whitcomb L. Judson. Have you heard of him? I certainly hadn't until I read an article specifically noting such unrecognized inventors. Judson, you see, invented *the zipper!*

Creativity is often thought of as some special quality only possessed by authors, artists and performers. But I believe Albert Einstein defined it best when he said, "Creativity is simply making something new or re-arranging the old in a new way." About his own accomplishments, he went on to say, "When I examined myself and my methods of thought, I came to the conclusion that the gift of fantasy has meant more to me than my talent for absorbing positive knowledge." In the previous chapter I described the work of a business consultant named Don Holmes, who interviewed the employees of troubled companies to get their viewpoints on how the company's problems might be solved. What astonished the executives of these companies, when they were presented with their employees' suggestions, was the incredible creativeness of people who were often only working in low-paying positions.

How to Enhance Creative Problem Solving

Dr. Herbert F. Crovitz, author of *The Creativity Question,* performs an experiment which is a classic in the psychology of problem solving. He drops a handful of corn on the ground in front of a hungry chicken. He then unobtrusively puts a transparent piece of plastic between the chicken and the corn. The chicken tries in vain to reach the corn directly through the transparent barrier, pecking the same way over and over again. It never occurs to the bird that all she has to do is go over or around the barrier. In Dr. Crowitz's terms, she is wearing a *relational filter* in front of her mind's eyes.

Our first impulse is to laugh at the stubborn chicken. When we look at other people's problems it is often clear to us that all they need to do to solve their problem is to approach it from a different direction—to change their viewpoint. Unfortunately, like the chicken, we are usually too close to our own problems to see them objectively. If our vision is "clouded" by emotion, we may not have the presence of mind to look at the situation rationally, from many different angles. Dr. Crowitz suggests using an aid to think about the problem from other viewpoints. One versatile tool is a list of the 42 *relation words* in basic English:

About	At	For	Of	Round	To
Across	Because	From	Off	So	Under
After	Before	If	On	Still	Up
Against	Between	In	Opposite	Then	When
Among	But	Near	Or	Though	Where
And	By	Not	Out	Through	While
As	Down	Now	Over	Till	With

If the chicken had had this list of words to check over, she might have tried "over" and "opposite" and been encouraged to jump over the barrier or to go around to the opposite side. In the midst of an emotional problem situation, the idea is that you can become more objective by checking the problem situation against the word list. Or you can use one of the checklists at the end of each of the chapters in this book.

Finding Solutions Through Creative Questioning

Alex F. Osborn, author of *Applied Imagination* and *Way Beyond the I.Q.*, developed a checklist for "inducing transformations." He suggests a basic list of eight action words like "substitute" and "rearrange." In my consulting practice I have been working for some time on an expanded list of similar action words to use in questions to stimulate solutions. I have found these to be extremely helpful in solving difficult problems. Try them on your own problem and see if they suggest a solution:

How could you . . .*(fill in with one of the following)*. . .

Adapt?	Amplify?	Rearrange?
Bypass?	Close?	Reverse?
Combine?	Distance?	Remove?
Divide?	Invert?	Substitute?
Lengthen?	Maximize?	Shorten?
Minify?	Modify?	Vary?
Narrow?	Open up?	Widen?

. . . your problem situation or attempted solution?

A KEY to solving problems quickly is to *ask yourself questions* which will stimulate creative thinking. If you can't think of any other creative question, answer the following two questions:

★   What could you do to *increase your own creative ability* so you could more effectively resolve your own problem?

★   What innovative person could you *employ* to dream up inspirational, creative strategies and solutions for you?

It may not always be possible to immediately find the right answers, but a good place to start is to come up with the right questions!

Why People Create Problems

At the beginning of every seminar I give, I ask if anyone has a pet cat. Generally someone has, so I ask him or her, "Do you have a 'scratching pole' for your cat?" Usually the answer is "yes," so I ask "Why do cats love to scratch? Why do they tear up your sofa or your drapes or your clothes if you don't provide them with a pole?" The answer, of course, is for the same reason dogs chew on bones, goats butt their heads against solid walls, bulls kick posts and woodpeckers peck on trees where there may be no insects to peck out. They are all *exercising* the tools which have been given them by Mother Nature as their weapons or tools for survival. They know instinctively they must keep these tools sharpened up or their survival may be at risk. They practice the use of these tools when no crisis is present so they will be in top form on the day when a real crisis is at hand.

Does Man perform a similar practice exercise with his "survival tool?" It is my contention that he does indeed! What is Man's "survival tool?" Obviously it is that characteristic of Man which enables him to ride in the wagon while the horse does the pulling. It is his brain, his mind, his superior *problem-solving* ability. Man is king of the animal kingdom because he can *out-think* all of the rest of the animals (or so we suppose). So what does Man do to "sharpen his tool," to be especially ready in a time of crisis? Why he *creates problems for himself to solve*, of course!

I'm not suggesting that every reader is creating every problem encountered in life. We all face the common problems of daily survival: obtaining food, clean water, clean air, shelter, love and companionship—all of the elements of Maslow's *Hierarchy of Needs*. Many people wrestle with problems of health or physical, mental or emotional handicaps. Throughout much of the world, unemployment and hunger are overwhelming problems. And yet in the face of these awesome problems, some people are able to create solutions, while others only seem to encounter additional problems. What makes the difference?

Why People With Problems Ignore Your Advice

In the business world you will hear it said that "if you're not part of the solution, you're part of the problem." Some people, it seems, are naturally "solvers" while others always seem to create problems. If you can *recognize* what part of a problem you are *creating*, you can begin to solve it more easily. By learning and applying problem-solving skills, you can eliminate those self-created elements and focus your *full* attention on the external, "real" elements of the problem.

I'm certain that many times you have observed the behavior of problem-creating people around you. You wondered why they did things which would obviously result in future problems for themselves. Why would anyone do something which would create problems and probably cost him or her days, weeks, or even years to straighten out? And, in many instances when warned by friends or family with an external, more objective point of view, why do they *ignore* good advice and insist on rushing headlong into the problem situation anyway? Are they simply stupid?

I propose that they are no more stupid than the cat who expends energy clawing on a post which will yield no benefit other than a bit of momentary clawing practice. They are instinctively creating problems to strengthen their minds and resourcefulness, to enhance their foremost survival tool! Eventually those of us who have survived long enough discover ways to deal with most of the problems which come our way. We no longer feel a need to create problems for ourselves. We have mastered most of the daily routines of life. And yet there are always larger problems to take on, if we so desire. As a species Mankind has only begun to solve the problems of human existence.

You may wonder why I would write this book at all if people are so determined to have problems and ignore suggested solutions. If they so fervently wish to solve their own problems, why would they bother to read a book like this? Fortunately there is an answer. While some people seem to *excel* at creating problems for themselves, they don't always do so well at *solving* them. What starts out to be a *challenging* experience, may turn out to be an *overwhelming* experience. When this occurs, the result can be a more open-minded approach to seeking solutions. Man has survived and stayed on top as long as he has by *turning to other minds* when he finds his own mind inadequate to resolve a problem at hand. The mark of mature creativity is the willingness to select creative elements from the works of others, and to add to those elements to form even more innovative solutions.

Learning Specific Problem Solving Skills

In ancient times, humans had to face the obvious problems of nature and simple survival. In today's complex society, there are many hidden facets to the problem situations in which we find ourselves. Every year, thousands of new entrepreneurs begin their first business enterprises. At the outset the apparency is that, with a little effort, they will realize great rewards. As they get deeper and deeper into the competitive world of commerce and trade, they may find they have "bitten off more than they can chew." It has been said that 90% of all new businesses fail. Many of those fail in the first year. What seemed at a distance to be quite a simple problem, up close became a very complex, apparently *unsolvable* problem.

Why do new businesses fail? Is it poor products? Insufficient capital? No, the reason for most of these business failures was not that their product wasn't good. Most even had enough capital to launch their new business *if they did things right.* It turns out that the most common reasons for failure are *poor management of resources* and *ineffective marketing, promotion and sales.*

Any of these problems could have been resolved by calling for competent professional help or by getting trained in these specialized areas. Why do entrepreneurs fail rather than seek effective help or learn better problem-solving procedures? Pride perhaps, or more likely they are unaware that they could be trained in the *skills of problem solving.*

An astute business-person wouldn't think for a moment of hiring someone to manage his or her bookkeeping or accounting records unless that person was very well trained in that field of expertise. Nor would legal problems be turned over to someone without a law degree and competence in the field of law. Astonishing though it may be however, that same business person may hire someone to *solve business problems* who had never had any formal training in *problem-solving procedure!* How can this be??? The simple answer is that formal training in problem-solving is not commonly available. It is not taught in grammar school, nor in high school nor even generally in most colleges. There are, of course, college courses in logic, and business courses which focus on solutions to specific categories of business problems. But, alas, for the vast multitudes, general problem solving training is not yet readily available. Only in recent years some of us in this field have begun to offer this information broadly through seminars, lectures and workshops, but there is a dire need for many more "Problem Solving Technique Trainers."

When a Solution Becomes a Problem

Peter Greene is a consultant who has specialized in training people in problem solving skills in many English-speaking countries around the world for more than twenty years. Currently he lives in Atlanta, Georgia, where he writes a column for a paper called *The New Age News.* In a recent column entitled "Solutions and Goals," Peter focused on a nasty phenomenon which occurs when the creative effort to solve a problem actually *creates additional problems!* Peter expressed the phenomenon so well in his article, I asked him for permission to reprint it in his own words:

Problems and solutions are opposite sides of the same coin. Often a problem you have today was once a solution, and the solutions you adopt today will shape tomorrow's problems. As with drugs and alcohol, what begins as a solution rapidly becomes a problem.

When I conducted a rehabilitation program in a prison I asked, "How many of you think you have a drug problem?" All hands went up. "That's the first error," I told them. "Actually you don't. You have a drug *solution!* That *solution* led to

HOW PEOPLE CREATE PROBLEMS
FROM A-TO-Z

Accepting without question
Blaming others
Challenging blindly
Delaying projects
Fabricating stories
Forgetting conveniently
Gambling compulsively
Hoping for the impossible
Ignoring other's ideas
Interrupting constantly
Jumping from project to project
Keeping poisonous company
Leaving incomplete task after task
Making unwarranted assumptions
Mumbling unintelligibly
Neglecting vital tasks
Never acknowledging others
Opposing any idea not one's own
Prevaricating
Quitting without completing
Retreating as standard policy
Stagnating—resisting change
Talking impulsively without listening
Unnecessarily risking
Vegetating—never looking ahead
Withholding information and help
eXperimenting at other's eXpense
Saying "Yes" when you should have said "No!"
Zapping others with no helpful intent

the problem of maintaining your habit. Your next solution was crime, which *led to your present problem* of being incarcerated. To stay out of jail you need to resolve the *original problem* that you *solved* by turning to drugs." Enlightenment permeated the room. The process of rehabilitation was begun — which incidentally had a notable success rate.

Another common example can be seen when young people feel stifled by their parents. Desiring freedom, they rush into premature marriages to get away from home. Then the solution of yesterday becomes the new problem. Some try to save their marriages by starting families. For a while having children may improve the situation, but the feeling of entrapment returns. Affairs, preoccupation with a career, an attempt to start a business, or finally getting a divorce may then be adopted as solutions.

Often from such "solutions," money becomes the next problem. Again the answer seems easy. Borrow or use charge cards. This generates future debt, solved by making minimum payments. The problem has not gone away. Temporarily dealt with, each "solution" becomes a new problem. In spite of a valiant struggle, the interest compounds and the debt grows bigger, but the *original desire for freedom from being stifled* is still there.

Bankruptcy beckons as a relief and a way out. "With divorce and bankruptcy behind you, you can make a fresh start," says you attorney (carefully ensuring that he gets paid in advance). If you do it, forget about buying a house or even a new car with "low down payment and your good credit." Bankruptcy is a "solution" that can haunt you for years. Wanting to be free, you forge new links in a chain of shackles with which to bind yourself.

This same pattern affects nations. Today's conflicts were born from the adoption of yesterday's diplomatic "solutions." Partitioning Korea and Viet Nam at the end of World War II later took America into two wars. Realize that an attempt to deal with your latest problem may be merely a continuation of a chain of problems and solutions and is not, in reality, a new problem. It is an old one in a new guise! When you find and vanquish the original basic problem, the chain will disappear and stay gone.

As Peter so aptly demonstrates, the desire to quickly *create* a solution often leads us to create *more problems*. By tracking back on a chain of attempted solutions, you will probably find the original objective. It may be a *growth* objective. Or, like Peter's example of the young adult leaving home to obtain freedom, it can be a *decline prevention* objective where one seeks to keep a bad situation from continuing or getting worse. At the beginning of such a sequence of failed "solutions" you will usually find a powerful desire. It's a creative urge into which you can breathe new life with the wisdom you have gained during your chain of bad "solutions."

You will frequently hear motivational speakers speak of "turning a lemon into lemonade." Can that occur when things have deteriorated this badly? Can you break this long chain of attempted solutions which have led to even more problems and perpetuated itself until you are totally dragged down, bound by this seemingly unbreakable chain? Yes. If you view this sequence of experiences as lessons in how *not* to solve the problem, you may be able to approach that original goal with renewed vigor and insight and truly create more than just a "solution." You may be able now to create a new reality, far better than what had even envisioned when you first sought to free yourself from that original problem.

Creating Problems or Solutions: The Choice Is Yours

Humans are naturally creative creatures. If they do not create in a controlled fashion, they create in an uncontrolled fashion. I think you will agree that people *create* problems for themselves, especially when their environment isn't challenging enough to keep their wits sharpened. One way to improve your ability to solve problems which you may have inadvertently or indirectly created, is to enhance your problem *creating* ability! This approach follows the logical premise that widening your *scope of address* will give you a wider perspective on the problem being addressed. How to do this? Try the following:

1. *Write down a new statement of your problem (keep noticing how your statement of the problem changes as you go along).*

2. *Create a scale of problem-solving difficulty, where you consider "1" to be the least difficult and "10" to be the most difficult. To establish the order of magnitude of a "10", write down the most difficult problem you can imagine. Do the same for a "1", writing down the least difficult problem you can imagine. Finally establish a "5" by describing a problem of "average" difficulty.*

3. *On that scale of 1 to 10, assign a degree of difficulty to your present problem.*

4. *(a) Think of someone else who has a problem of about the <u>same degree of difficulty</u> and note it down. (b) Think of someone who has a problem of <u>slightly greater difficulty</u>*

and note that down. (c) Think of someone who has a problem of lesser difficulty and note that down.

5. *Now imagine* (don't be real) *a problem which is of exactly the same degree of difficulty as the one you have. Then do it again. Continue creating imaginary problems until you notice that you have acquired a new perspective on your own problem.*

(Add any new solving technique that you think of to your list in back of the book.)

Creating a Master Plan

Of the five stages in the problem solving sequence, *input, verify, design, test* and *output*, or *apply*, the most critical is *design*. It is at this point that you turn from collecting and verifying information and resources and begin to formulate the actions needed to arrive at a solution. When solving small problems, this phase may occur so quickly you're not even aware of it. Take this simple example: Like most people, you have probably locked your key in your car a few times. The problem solving steps were direct and simple. The *input* stage consisted of noticing the door was locked and the keys were inside. You *verified* the problem by walking around the car, trying all of the other doors until you were satisfied that you were indeed locked out. Now it was time to *design* a solution. In the days when cars were still locked by pressing down a large stem near the door handle, you could work a coat hanger through the window and then down to lift the stem and unlock the door. All you had to do was find a hanger. With today's more subtle locking mechanisms, your solution design would probably have to include calling a locksmith. In either case the design phase of solving was so obvious it probably took only a few seconds.

Although the simplest of problems may sometimes defy finding a simple solution, more often the complex problems are the ones which give you the most trouble. You live in a complex world where it is nearly impossible for you to know enough about every aspect of life to solve all of your problems yourself. Much of the time in college courses is spent teaching students *where to find information*. It is already assumed that they will not remember all of the facts they will need in business, medicine, law, science, or other complex disciplines. A more valuable skill in our modern world is *knowing how to find facts quickly* when you need them. When you finish this book you will have absorbed much information

MASTER SOLUTION DESIGN

Copyright 1988, Thomas B. Franklin — OCTAGON PRESS, Box 36854, Los Angeles, CA 90036

OCTAGON FACTORS	INPUT (Elements)	VERIFY (Feasibility)	DESIGN (Sequence)	TEST (Simulate)	APPLY (Implement)
MORALE & MOTIVATION	WHY? Your purpose and commitment!	Check probability of win or loss	Overall sequence of master plan	Simulate risks & contingency plan	Written statement of goal commitment
HELP EXCHANGE	WHO? To help? Will they help or harm?	Can you really help & inspire support?	Sequence of help & seeking help	Rehearse delivery of help & asking	Give & receive help as planned
KNOWLEDGE ABILITY	WHAT–Facts?Ideas skills, info?	Check facts, ideas info & skill needed	HOW? To learn facts, skills, info.?	Practice getting & monitoring info flow	Gather facts, ideas skills, information
COMMUNICATION EXCHANGE	WHAT? Needs to be communicated?	Check possibility of comm. give & take	Best sequence of comm. exchanges	Rehearse delivering comm. & listening	Announce plan & deliver comm.
RESOURCES FINANCE	WHAT:People, space finances & equip.?	Check applicability availability & cost	HOW? To obtain? to employ? to use?	Test workability, sufficiency, quality	Obtain resources & finances per plan
EXPANSION OR GROWTH	Into WHAT: Space? role–market–level?	Check risks & expansion feasibility	Plan sequence of expansion steps	Simulate to test risk of loss or win	Begin move into new role & spaces
CREATIVITY & PERSPECTIVE	Ideas & variations: previous solutions	Check feasibility of creative variations	Sequence–applied creative ideas	Simulate or dummy– run new ideas	Put creative ideas into action
PRODUCTIVE OUTPUT	Systems & tech. for faster action	Check feasibility of techniques	Plan sequence of action steps.	Simulate & test action sequence	Carry out plan of action & review

on problem-solving, but it is unlikely that you will remember all of it. Also, because serious problems create added emotional stress, you may be even *less likely* to think of these solving techniques when you most need them. The *checklists* at the end of most of the chapters in this book should help overcome this problem. Ideally you should keep them close at hand to refer to when you encounter a difficult problem.

To assist you in the design of a master solution for any problem, I have provided you with a "Master Plan Design" chart. It is quite abbreviated but it should provide somewhat of a framework for you to build on. You will notice that the *stages of solving* head up columns across the chart, and the *Octagon Factors* (eight major divisions of life or business), are put in eight rows down along the left-hand side of the chart. You may also notice that to aid you in designing both the *input* and the *output* sides of a solution more easily, I have set up the *Octagon Factors* in input/output pairs. When you analyze the solving strategies of some of the "Super-Solvers" mentioned earlier in this book, you will find they have used these input/output pairs to great advantage without even realizing it.

Morale & Motivation -- Help Exchange

Enthusiastic, motivated people seem to naturally seek to help others. Motivation and enthusiasm for an endeavor are the first prerequisites for success. If you're not really motivated to solve a problem, you probably won't. In Chapter Four, I introduced you to Bonnie MacAllister, a former winner of the "Small Business Person of the Year" award. In an interview with *Success* magazine, Bonnie noted that she had about twenty jobs before she started her own business. She worked as a receptionist, secretary, manager and sales-person, but she didn't find what she was looking for by working as an employee. By that time she was strongly motivated to "do her own thing." In business, the best received products and services are those which fill a real need; they are products or services which really *help* a client or customer in some unique way. Naturally the profits from the sale of the service or product also *help* the seller, therefore there is a real *exchange* of help.

When Bonnie, with the help of her chemist, created a new polymer artificial fingernail, not only did she develop a product which was more glamorous and far more durable than the acrylic nails which had existed up until that time, but she created a very strong nail which resisted even the most "hard-core nail-biter." Bonnie says, "We're offering a superior product, and, to the best of my knowledge, nobody has ever enjoyed the kind of success we've had with our process." For women who really needed Bonnie's product, it was indeed a great *help!* Bonnie's powerful desire to create her own business motivated her to find a product that women would immediately *recognize* as uniquely helpful.

Knowledge & Ability -- Communication Exchange

R. David Thomas, who coined the *Kentucky Fried Chicken* name and image for Colonel Sanders and went on to found the *Wendy's Old Fashioned Hamburgers* chain, was also a highly motivated individual. He says, "Since I was 12, I've wanted to be in the burger business." David's father was a construction worker, traveling from job to job. Dave began working part time jobs early in life, and at the age of twelve he was already frying hamburgers at a local grill. His education in various kitchens continued until he enlisted in the army at the age of seventeen, and it was there that he was trained as a cook. When he was shipped to a base in Germany, he became the youngest soldier ever to run a non-commissioned officer's club. At that point he learned an important lesson which he carried forward into every restaurant venture in which he has been involved. His success in solving the problems of running a popular club, he says, was "just making sure the NCO club was clean, the food was good and the service fast."

Knowledge is gained through communication is mainly *input*. The real problem solving power of knowledge comes from communicating that knowledge to others. Dave Thomas first communicated his knowledge of how to run a fast, clean, efficient enterprise in his management position with Colonel Sanders. He repeated that success in his position as vice president of operations for Arthur Treacher's *Fish & Chips*, which he helped get moving at the very start. Finally he polished that success as founder of his own *Wendy's* chain.

As the popularity of the *Wendy's* chain grew, it became necessary to develop personnel policies which would take the drudgery out of mass hamburger production. This was accomplished in *Wendy's* by a special form of transmitting knowledge through communication called *cross-training*. Every line employee was trained to perform equally well as cashier, grill-man, sandwich-maker, busboy and order-coordinator. In an industry where the problem of job-stagnation results in an annual 300 percent turnover, *Wendy's* turnover was as low as 50 percent in one year! Creative techniques communicated well through effective training made the difference.

Motivation and help are also high on David's list of important qualities. He says, "This is the only country where a busboy who didn't finish high school can make it like this. *People can do anything they want to if they set their goals high enough."* His viewpoint on help is *"Always put more back into life than what you take out."* In the past he has backed up that statement by sponsoring a special TV charity drive to combat catastrophic childhood diseases, and an annual Easter Seals telethon which has raised more than a quarter million dollars in a single year.

Resources & Finance -- Growth & Expansion

Before we leave David Thomas's story, it is interesting to note that he moved from a level of solving the problems which came his way while running a *single* eating establishment, to solving the problems of a faltering string of six Colonel Sander's restaurants, to solving the problems of running nearly two thousand *Wendy's*. He followed the natural sequence of accumulating greater wealth and resources, and then investing that wealth to create *growth and expansion*. But Thomas continued expanding beyond the realm of business endeavors. This is apparent from his attempts to try to solve larger social problems, through events like his telethons.

So far the problem solving strategies designed by these "Super-Solvers" have been rather routine and predictable. Increased knowledge opens up a potential for greater communication power. An increase in resources generally leads to a greater capability for expansion. *Creative* problem solving, however, calls for an innovative twist on conventional methods. Consider the approach of this "Super-Solver": Wally Amos, founder of "Famous Amos Chocolate Chip Cookies," was the first black agent for the industry-leading William Morris Agency. He handled super stars like Simon and Garfunkle, The Supremes, Marvin Gaye and Dionne Warwick. In running his chocolate chip business, he worked *backwards,* using his *marketing expansion* techniques to build the necessary *resources* and capital.

By the beginning of this decade, *Famous Amos* was selling four hundred pounds of cookies a day and grossing over a million dollars a year. Using his marketing skills as an agent, Amos arranged appearances for his cookies on "The Mike Douglas Show," "Good Morning America," and "Not for Women Only." As an experienced promoter, Wally never missed a chance to use promotional gimmicks. He offers Famous Amos T-Shirts, Famous Amos Kazoos and a single record, "Wally's Theme." Like Dave Thomas, Wally Amos contributes to the community by providing cookies for just about any charity group that asks. His very creative and professional approach to marketing expansion has turned what could have been no more than the specialty item of a local cookie store in Hollywood, into a nationally recognized product!

Thomas J. Watson Sr. had already purchased the patents for the "punch card," and then the patents for a time clock, before World War I. At the beginning of World War II his company, IBM, was a small, struggling business equipment company. Watson, however, had a grand future in mind for his company. It was reflected in his choice of the name: "International Business Machines," although his company was far from international at the time.

Watson's subsequent success came from a number of highly creative innovations. The first of these was Watson's change in how assembly line workers defined their tasks. Watson discovered that workers were often idle on the assembly line because they were waiting for an advance set-up man. He immediately viewed this situation as a problem to be solved and determined to try an innovative solution. By re-training his workers to do their own set-up, and eventually their own inspection, he combined several skills in one worker and greatly increased the efficiency of the assembly line. This led eventually to re-defining the role of the supervisor. At IBM the foreman is called an "assistant" and his or her job is to provide workers with materials, tools and information. This innovation also solved problems of training, turnover, and supervisor/worker hostility.

The second major innovation which set IBM apart from the competition was also a response to a problem situation. In the late forties, when the first electronic computers were being developed, there was an urgent demand for the product which forced IBM to begin production before the engineering had been completed. This meant that the engineers had to work with the foremen and workers on the production floor to put together the final details of the design, the production layout, and individual job setups. This was the first time the worker had an opportunity to get in on the planning of, and design of, not only a product, but also the production process and, to some degree, his own job. The results of this forced experiment were unexpected. The design was superior, production engineering was significantly faster and more cost-efficient, and the individual workers were notably more productive with greater satisfaction in product output.

In creating the design of a master plan to solve a long-term problem, it is *vital* to involve everyone connected with the problem. People vary greatly in their degree of creative imagination, but no knows a specific job better than the person doing it from day to day. Production management in Communist countries has been a dismal failure because the design has been imposed from the top down, rather than being drawn from the wisdom and knowledge of the workers at the action end of the line.

How can you translate this idea into an immediate creative solution for your own problem? Look down the "Input" and "Verify" columns on the "Master Plan Design" chart. In the previous chapter on *Communication Power,* I told you about Don Holmes and his interviewing method of solving company problems. The KEY to his success was his ability to draw out the facts and suggested solutions from *everyone involved* in any aspect of the problem area. The creative ideas which emerged through his interviews amazed top management. This technique of drawing on all creative powers available is partly what has made IBM the success it is today.

Don't neglect your own creative inspiration, but also don't neglect the potential creative input you can obtain from those around you who are willing to help. The quality of your end product solution may be astonishingly better.

Defining Your Role as Solution Designer

You will recall that some of the synonyms of "define" were "set limits," "set boundaries," and "separate out." For each of the five phases of problem solving you have a different role to play—a different hat to wear. In the beginning you wear the hat of "collector." You gather facts, opinions, helpful information and resources. Then your job changes. You become the "verifier," checking the facts, confirming your sources and verifying your resources. Up to this point your tasks were mainly administrative, although you probably had to exercise some creativity to get the information you needed out of a few reluctant people or organizations. Now, however, your task becomes mainly creative. You have assembled the elements of the problem. It is time to use those elements to fashion a solution.

It has been said that, "the best laid plans of mice and men oft go astray." The saying may be an old one, but the experience is as contemporary as a MacDonald's hamburger. How often have you carefully planned a day's activities or perhaps a trip with several stops. On your checklist the plan looked perfectly plausible, but when you got out and began to go from place to place, unexpected events got in your way. A traffic jam messed up your time schedule. Perhaps a store or office you went to was unexpectedly closed. An item you had taken to be repaired wasn't ready yet. The list goes on and on. Our best laid plans often fall apart in the real world.

There are some measures you can take to increase the probability that your designed solution will work, even if the specific steps of the plan don't fall in place exactly as you intended. The first step is to *separate out* the roles you play, the hats you wear, the jobs you must do. The most effective way to do this is to *separate the spaces and times* in which you work for each of these jobs. When gathering and verifying facts, this usually happens automatically. You have to travel around to gather information, and you have to set aside a definite time to call people or see them. When it comes time to *create* a solution, however, few people consider the importance of doing it in the right setting.

Creativity can be a fragile ability. Talk to any writer and they will tell you of the horror of "writer's block." If you have written term papers for school or college you may have encountered the frustration of sitting down to write and drawing a mental blank. I can't guarantee that doing what I am about to suggest will always enable you to come up with instant creative inspiration, but I can guarantee that you will be less distracted and thus have more of your attention creatively focused.

The perfect creative environment will vary from person to person. An artist painting a garbage dump may find that dump the perfect place to create. Personally, I find it difficult, if not impossible, to think creatively in a cluttered or distracting space. If I am about to compose a creative work, I either clean up my office so I don't have incomplete projects and papers lying around to distract me, or I go off to the park or up on a mountain where I am surrounded by nature and have an aesthetic view. I make certain that I will not be interrupted by the phone and I ask friends and family not to disturb me during a period of concentrated creativity. When I write, I am most creative in the morning, before the day's distractions begin, or in the evening when the day's obligations have ended.

Think about your own situation. When is the best time for you to create? Do you have a private space where you can concentrate without interruptions? If not, can you get a library card and work there, or sign up for a study room at a local school? Don't neglect the selection of a comfortable place to create. Few great artists or composers created a fine work of art without a private studio or space to work in. If you are working on a solution to a major problem, give yourself a break. Design your solution where you can give that design your full attention.

Defining the Worker Roles

Once you have designed a master plan, it is time to get specific about the steps and who will carry them out. You may consider this part of the same activity, but I'd like you to consider, for a moment, treating this next step as a totally different activity. Remember that a major premise I presented at the beginning of this book was that the natural divisions of labor in business also apply to the way you define and divide your efforts in personal problem-solving. In large corporations, major strategies are decided upon by the top executives. Once these strategies have been spelled out in general, they are passed down to managers, who work out specific assignments and designate projects and tasks for those employees most qualified to work on them.

I am a list-writer. My days are filled with such diverse activities that I wouldn't stand a chance of doing all that I have planned without a detailed list. Some people hate lists. Others hate to write down anything at all. Perhaps a creative alternative for such people is a tape recorder. In the movie *Nightshift*, starring Shelly Long and Michael Keaton, the character played by Keaton carries around a tape recorder and whenever inspiration strikes, he records it on the spot. In the film this activity becomes hysterically funny, but in real life you may find that playing back a tape recording of you itemizing your planned actions would work well—perhaps even better than a written list.

There is another important reason why it is best to have a written or recorded "recipe" for carrying out the steps of your plan. Recall my recommendation for you to create your master design in a private, distraction-free space. Let us suppose you have taken my suggestion and worked out your plan on a hilltop, in aesthetic seclusion. Now here you are, working on some step of the plan amidst the hustle and bustle of daily business or traffic. Faced with added chaos and confusion, it is easy to lose the clear, calm vision you had on the mountaintop when you were designing your master strategy. You can suddenly find yourself making compromises and unwise alterations if you allow yourself to wear your "creator" hat while you're being a *worker*. If you see a need to modify your plan, make a note of it, as a worker would. Put it in your mental "suggestion box," but don't make a change in the master strategy until you are back in a distraction-free, creative "ivory tower." Keep the jobs of *creator, manager* and *worker* separated out. You will have a much better chance of designing a good plan and getting that plan carried out effectively.

Work With the Grain -- Not Against It

Around the turn of the century, Oliver Wendell Holmes Jr. said, "Life is painting a picture, not doing a sum." My observations have convinced me that creative imagination is indeed a more valuable tool for solving personal problems than mathematical precision. I do believe, however, that chiseling a scupture is a better simile than painting a picture. When painting a picture, the artist has control over all of the elements. He or she can choose any canvas, paints and brushes desired. The sculptor, on the other hand, must live with certain fixed qualities in the medium, whether it is stone, wood or metal. When working with wood, the sculptor must deal with the natural grain. Stone has been developed, layer upon layer, over the years. Once again, the sculptor must work with the grain that exists in the medium. The sculpture is a blend of the artist's intent and what the medium will allow.

And so we are back to the "best laid plans" which often go astray. The solution designer must realize that, while the overall strategy can be firmly established, the steps must remain as fluid as the sculptor's chisel. In carrying out the steps of the plan, there must be alternative routes in the event that the chosen path is closed. To create an optimum effect, it is usually best to work "with the grain" rather than against it. The master designer strives to superimpose an ideal design on the real world. Whether painting a picture, chiseling a sculpture, or solving a problem, achieving this balance is a true work of art.

From Creating Problems to Creating Solutions

A final approach to developing creative problem solving ability is to use *intelligence enhancement techniques*. These can *stretch* your thinking ability, expand your creativity, and possibly increase your measurable I.Q. My own background would hardly seem to qualify me to be a "professional solver," or to write this book. I began my undergraduate work at Chicago Teacher's College, and obtained a certificate to teach music from Manner's Conservatory of Music in Chicago, Illinois. My early education was therefore in Music rather than in any field of study which addresses formal problem solving.

Then my life completely turned around while I was in the military in the early 1960s. I learned of some new research into processes which could greatly increase human intelligence, reaction time, and performance ability. The group which had reported these processes had submitted five hundred test scores to the Office of Naval Research, showing I.Q. increases of from ten to fifty points. By 1966, the U.S. Army Research Institute, The National Science Foundation, and the U.S. Office of Naval Research began to jointly fund an annual symposium held by the International Association for the Study of Attention and Performance. But even before that I was irresistably attracted to the experimental program showing dramatic I.Q. increases. I had attended ten different schools during my twelve years in grammar school and high school, and some subjects remained quite difficult for me. As a result of my participation in this program, I took the I.Q. tests offered by Mensa, the high I.Q. society, and found I had experienced an I.Q. increase of 30 points. I had qualified to join Mensa.

That increase in I.Q. changed my life dramatically. I went back to college and, where before I had gotten B's and C's, I now had nearly straight A's. I began to investigate the procedures which had produced this major improvement in such a short time. The exercises had consisted mainly of drills in attention control, communication skills, and question and answer processes. I could see that, because of a lack of these skills, people *create* problems for themselves rather than solving them. They do this by:

• Not listening carefully enough.
• Not evaluating what they hear quickly enough.
• Not arriving at correct decisions quickly enough to take advantage of existing opportunities.
• Not getting their information or their point across to others clearly.
• Not disciplining their attention and maintaining a firm focus on the problem at hand.
• Not following through and completing what they start (or not decisively abandoning futile or unproductive projects).

When I realized that I.Q. tests test specific skills, it became obvious that exercises which developed these skills would result in an increase in I.Q. Note some of the skills commonly tested by I.Q. tests, and look at some of the ways in which you can use this problem solving text and recommended techniques to improve your own skills:

• They test how quickly you can grasp a question or problem and go to work on answering or solving it. *(You can use this text to speed-up your problem analysis skills!)*.
• They test how quickly you can differentiate solvable from unsolvable problems and how well you can concentrate on the solvable problems. *(You can use the checklists at the end of each chapter to more readily identify solvable problems!)*.
• They test how quickly you can access the facts and processes in your memory which you need to arrive at an answer or solution. *(You can learn to focus FIRST on solving problems which are distracting your attention and muddying your thought processes!)*.
• They test how quickly you can arrive at, and state an answer to, one question or problem, and then move on to the next.

(You can use the principle of focusing ALL of your attention on one problem at a time. Never stop working on a solution without either completing it, delegating it, or re-scheduling it, while you locate additional information or resources).

In general, I.Q. tests provide questions and problems which can be solved by people with an average education. It would be possible for many more people to make high scores *if they can could think more quickly!* Tests are timed, thus *speed of thought and solution* determine I.Q. scores to a greater degree than educational background. If a reader really applies the problem solving techniques in this text, he or she may experience an actual improvement in perception and intelligence! The ultimate test is whether you are able to *actively use* these creative techniques to increase your ability to solve problems, and to sharpen that wonderful survival tool you possess: your intelligence and wit.

The Incredible Problem Solving Power of Your Own Creativity

I have called your attention to the fact that Man's primary survival tool is his mind, and it is his problem solving ability which sets him above the rest of the animal kingdom. I would go a step further and say that the way in which Man most closely approaches a *god-like* nature, is his *creative* ability. Man is, above all, a *creative* being. Whatever he can conceive of in his mind, it seems he will attempt to create in the physical world.

It also seems that to remain psychologically and emotionally healthy, people need to have a creative outlet. Wherever they go, humans leave their creative mark, even though in many instances we consider it graffiti. Some popular ways of creating an image include bumper stickers, signs hanging in cars, messages printed on T-shirts or tatooed on arms and chests, initials carved in trees or scribbled on sidewalks, and signs hung in bathrooms or kitchens or offices. On a more elaborate scale, Man leaves his creative mark in his buildings, his bridges, his parks, his highways, and his sculptures, like Mount Rushmore. Just about everywhere you go on this planet you will find Man's creative mark, and now you will even find his flags flying on the moon.

If you wish to discourage and depress a human, place him or her in a sterile environment and forbid the making of a mark or the hanging of a sign on any wall or surface. When employees are prevented from contributing suggestions and creating effects in the workplace, they become apathetic or destructive. When children are prevented from making creative changes in the space around them, they too become apathetic or destructive. I have no evidence to support this view, but it seems to me that when Man cannot create, he will often choose to destroy. Somehow Man has the need to *alter* his surroundings, his environment, his universe. If he can't alter it for the better, then he'll alter it for the worse. This is especially true of children. If you don't channel their creative energies in a constructive direction, they are certain to break something or tear something down. I believe the same is true with adults. It's just not as obvious.

Use your creativity power to create solutions, not problems. The world is full of problems to be solved. Problems tend to persist because of a lack of fresh, innovative thinking, which could lead to effective, creative solutions. There is never a scarcity of challenges to meet. When you have mastered your personal problems, take on the problems of a larger sphere around you. The techniques presented in this book will work for problems of any magnitude, from the problems of a child in grammar school, to the problems of a world leader striving for world peace and abundance. The techniques work well. Please use them.

PROBLEM SOLVING POWER

CHECKLIST NUMBER NINE

— Energize —

Creative solutions are mainly untried, untested, actions which, if unsuccessful, will be called "errors," and which, if successful, will probably be called "a stroke of genius."

To solve problems more effectively, how could you....

1 - Create a solution in terms of your objective? What ideal situation would you create if this problem was not preventing you from being what you wish to be? Doing what you want to do? Obtaining what you wish to obtain?

2 - Create ways to go over, around, behind or through obstacles standing in the way of you being what you wish to be? Doing what you wish to do? Obtaining what you wish to acquire?

3 - Make your resources do double, triple or quadruple duty? Find a creative way to (legally) obtain the use of other's resources? Creatively multiply your solving resources?

4 - Devise new and creative solving strategies? Break out of unwanted, stagnant, uncreative patterns?

5 - Create ways to combine learning with conversation or fun? Create clever questions to obtain information you need to resolve your problems? Creatively challenge assumptions? Find new ways to verify facts?

6 - Devise a strategy to fit more morale-building activities into your schedule? Invent a way to maintain a healthier diet without being hungry—to exercise more without being bored or exhausted—to feel less unhappy and more enthusiastic—to complete what you start?

7 - Find a creative way to tactfully give help to a "problem person," to both his or her advantage and yours as well? Think of new ways to compliment, advise or even criticize problem people without being destructive or offensive?

8 – Create more interesting and productive conversations? Create more interesting questions to find out how others have used their resources and solved their problems? Listen more creatively and speak more effectively?

9 – Creatively maximize your use of time? Cleverly schedule productive activities so you accomplish more? Put tentative solutions into action to test them?

10 - Create innovative approaches to expanding into new spaces? Relationships? Jobs? Markets? Environments? Activities? Projects? Solutions?

11 - Create a new context for your life where what now seems to be a problem, becomes an opportunity to change and grow?

12 - Use an existing problem situation to inspire the creation of an entirely new approach to solving this kind of problem?

(a) Use several words from this list of the 42 *relation words* in basic English, in your statements of tentative solutions:

About	At	For	Of	Round	To
Across	Because	From	Off	So	Under
After	Before	If	On	Still	Up
Against	Between	In	Opposite	Then	When
Among	But	Near	Or	Though	Where
And	By	Not	Out	Through	While
As	Down	Now	Over	Till	With

(b) Consider one of the following actions to change your viewpoint on your problem situation. What would happen?

Adapt?	*Amplify?*	*Rearrange?*
Bypass?	*Close?*	*Reverse?*
Combine?	*Distance?*	*Remove?*
Divide?	*Invert?*	*Substitute?*
Lengthen?	*Maximize?*	*Shorten?*
Minify?	*Modify?*	*Vary?*
Narrow?	*Open up?*	*Widen?*

Rigid rules and doctrines keep people from thinking in new directions and arriving at creative solutions.

*Unsolved problems are often attributed to a scarcity
of resources. In actual fact, there is no scarcity
of resources—only an unwillingness to
search far enough for them.*

10. RESOURCE POWER

Resource: 1. Something that can be turned to for support or help. 2. An available supply that can be drawn upon when needed. 4. Means that can be used to advantage. 5. Available capital; assets. (Capital: Any form of material wealth used, or available for use, in the production of more wealth.)
—*American Heritage Dictionary*

Resource Problem Definition: *Many problems could be viewed as an absence or scarcity of some <u>resource</u> (or an excess of some unwanted "resource").*
(Note: Often people or organizations don't solve problems because they don't bring <u>all</u> of the resources at their disposal to bear on the problem.)

The most frequently stated reason for an unsolved problem is a lack of resources—usually money. Many business owners state that if they had more capital for equipment, plant expansion, or more employees, then their major problems would vanish. Up and coming business executives tell us that if they had money to dress better, drive a better car, and perhaps take some additional college courses or training programs, they would be more successful and have fewer problems. Parents say that if they had more money to spend on their children, their children would be less of a problem to them. Some of these people may be right. Most of them are wrong. They don't have the problem because of a lack of resources. They only seem to have a lack of resources because of a failure to use their resources effectively.

A Simple Program for Solving Resource Problems:

Financial resource problems are the most common and the simplest to solve. They can usually be solved by doing the following:

1. Do a thorough inventory of all resources available.
2. List what resources are actually needed to resolve the current problem.
3. Identify any dormant assets that could be liquidated to pay outstanding debts or acquire needed resources. Do so.
4. Identify what resources are being wasted, and what expenses could be trimmed. Determine how unpaid bills might be paid with existing income. Do whatever is necessary to bring these expenses under control.
5. Identify what skills, talents, equipment, and other production capabilities are not being fully used. Utilize these resources more completely for producing income.

6. Set up an expansive training program to greatly increase the production, sales and delivery skills of existing personnel, including yourself.

7. Set up a production-reward system, which effectively motivates your income producers to put out that *extra* effort needed to increase income above outgo in the organization. Remove any penalties for high production.

8. Find an external source of any additional resources needed. Send out a persuasive request for those resources and persist until you get them.

These steps may not be easy to put into practice, but if you persist in applying them, they will eventually enable you to remedy most of your actual resource problems. Problems are seldom the result of insufficient resources. The needed resources are available if you look long enough and far enough. Often you already have them, but have not yet realized that fact.

Paper Work: The Unavoidable Essential to Control Resources

Economics has been called "the dismal science", in part because it can be a very dry, unromantic activity. Only a very few individuals find accounting or bookkeeping to be exciting. Most of us procrastinate, even on balancing our checkbooks, and only a small percentage of people in the population could tell you, offhand, what their net worth is. Nevertheless, your first step must be to do an inventory. Find out exactly what you do have and what you don't have. It will be worth the effort. I would expect most people reading this chapter to be yawning loudly by now, and few readers will finish the chapter without an interesting story interjected at this point. It usually takes a call from the I.R.S. to really get people to put their financial records in place in a hurry, although some people may be motivated by an opportunity to get a loan at extremely low interest. Our society is, individually, the most deeply indebted society in history. We have moved from a society of frugal individuals with strong savings accounts to a society of debtors with very few solvent citizens. Government policies have encouraged this state of affairs for many years by taxing income and encouraging consumer spending. In this way they reward consumption and discourage production. The government encourages debt by granting deductions for interest on loans, and it penalizes people for saving by taxing their savings accounts, or by permitting financial institutions to pay interest rates barely larger than the rate of inflation. The result is a gigantic increase in loans and debt, and a great decrease in savings accounts. People respond to rewards and penalties, and only the most determined individual will stay solvent despite incentives to do the opposite.

If you find you have buried yourself in a pile of debt, start unpiling yourself by finding out where you stand. Then organize a program to gradually move into a solvent position, with little or no debt and a positive cash flow.

There Really is No Scarcity of Resources

If your problem seems to be the result of a lack of resources, especially money, the first remedial rule is:

Put your full attention on income and production. Completely take your attention off from consumption and spending.

The second rule is:

Put your attention on what you DO have, not on what you DON'T have!

These two rules will carry you a long way toward remedying any real or imagined "scarcity of resources."

I refer to "scarcity of resources" rather facetiously, because in the long run, *there is no scarcity of resources!* In America, and in much of the Western World, we live in the midst of the wealthiest societies ever to exist. Only the poorest immigrants, slum dwellers, and street people lack even a television set. While hunger is still a problem for some of our older, mentally ill, or displaced poor, government food stamp programs and private charities, like the Salvation Army, supply supplemental food to tens of thousands across the U.S. Compared to totalitarian regimes such as Ethiopia, where the government currently *prevents* people from obtaining food, people in our country have an overwhelming abundance of food. And food is not the only resource we have in great abundance in this wealthiest of societies.

There is a hidden benefit to doing the first step on my simple resource scarcity correction list:

Do a thorough inventory of all resources available.

When asked to total up *all* resources, most people list only *their own* bank accounts, investment assets, cars, furniture, houses, tools or business places. In most states, we pay a sales tax on everything we purchase and, at the end of each year, we also pay income taxes. Part of that tax money is used to buy resources. As a taxpayer, you are a part owner of those resources. The streets, the sidewalks, the highways, the parks, the libraries, the beaches, the public galleries, the city, county, state and federal halls of records—all of these are facilities you have at your immediate disposal. And this is only a beginning.

Some people might object that there is little personal value in these public resources because of the fact that we have *restrictions* on our use of them. We can only go to the library or halls of public records during the hours they are open. If we wish to exercise our access to the Library of Congress or the Smithsonian Museum, we have to travel to Washington, D.C. But then I never said you wouldn't have to *do anything* to take advantage of the many resources available to you.

If you are willing to include, in your inventory, resources to which you have only limited access, then you can include riches beyond the dreams of the wealthiest sultan. Consider some of the places you have available to view any time you choose. For most people the house or business building they own is a special work of art. You will usually find, in front of every well-kept private home, a crisply cropped lawn surrounded by carefully planted and pruned bushes or flowers. An attractive walk-way is frequently added, and the porch or facade of the house is designed to make the overall appearance of the entrance inviting to any visitor or guest. People take pride in their dwelling places, and spend lavishly to paint and decorate to provide a pleasing visual experience for even those who simply drive or walk by. Even in the poorest neighborhoods, I have seen small houses so beautifully decorated, they looked like works of art.

Our freedom to view the artistry of dwelling places isn't limited to common neighborhoods. We have free access to the richest neighborhoods in our nation. Here in California, where I currently live, I can drive by and, on special tours, even *visit* the homes of the stars. The mansions of Beverly Hills and the surrounding areas are magnificent to behold. This is a visual resource immediately available to all who live here, not to mention the many parks, museums, galleries, libraries and malls. If a lack of some resource is causing your problem to persist, it may be time to take another look at the availability of that resource.

The Space Factor in Resource Power

Probably you're asking, "How much does this really have to do with solving my problems?" In the earlier chapter on *Creativity*

Power, you were asked to look at your problem from every imaginable viewpoint. One of your greatest resources is *space.* In our nation you have boundless space. Unlike a totalitarian state, where you must have special papers to travel, here you have an unlimited right to go anywhere in the nation. Somewhere, someone in this nation has had the same problem you have, or one very much like it. And it is very likely that someone has *solved* the very problem that you have.

One of the great perpetrators of problems is **fixity:** *the quality or condition of being fixed: firmly in position; stationary; unmovable.* A major problem in society is unemployment. Factories and offices close down leaving vast numbers of unemployed people in the community where the employer was located. Other jobs may be available in a wide range of locations hundreds or even thousands of miles away, but the difficulty of moving keeps many people from going where the work is. To find the solution to a problem it is often necessary to change locations, to get another viewpoint on the problem.

Space also influences how we think and who we think we are. Dress like a bum and go down to skid row and you'll probably feel like part of the gang. Dress in your finest and walk through the finest neighborhoods or shopping centers, and you should feel substantially better. If you have had a problem in your home or office and you stay there wearing the same clothes you did when you had the problem, it is likely that you will stay *fixed* in the problem viewpoint. Ask yourself: How would a person dress, who had solved this problem? Where would a person go, who had solved this problem? Try dressing that way and going to those places. Watch people who have solved the problem that seems so difficult for you to resolve. They are an excellent resource for you to draw on to become a *solver.*

Copying Success

A relatively new approach to personal improvement is known as "NLP": *Neuro-Linguistic-Programming.* A highly effective technique used by NLP is called "modeling." NLP defines it as "The process of discovering the sequence of internal representations (pictures, sounds, feelings, smells, tastes) and behaviors which enable someone to accomplish a task." Stated more simply, it means that if you observe someone who is extremely competent at a skill, like golf, archery or skiing, and you may find out *exactly* how that person uses strategy, language, beliefs and behavior to perform so well. Then, by painstakingly duplicating every aspect of that person's approach to the skill, you can come close to performing equally as well.

Anthony Robbins, author of *Unlimited Power,* a popular book on NLP, tells of using "modeling" to train a group of military trainees in effective marksmanship. According to Robbins, the military has had a problem with poor trainee marksmanship, and the usual training techniques have not been effective. NLP trainers first studied top marksmen to find out what they saw, heard, and did, both internally and externally. They then got the trainees to duplicate, as closely as possible, each inner and outer stance of the top marksmen. The result was a dramatic increase in trainee marksmanship. NLP "modeling" is a real test of your powers of observation. It forces you to "input" the totality of every resource being employed by a successful solver.

In *The Inner Game of Tennis,* author and tennis coach Timothy Gallwey stresses learning by watching, by visualizing what has been seen, and by allowing the body to simply execute what has been perceived. He provides the model of a properly executed tennis movement. Through his "yoga tennis" approach to teaching, he often enables students to learn in a single lesson what normally takes weeks using conventional tennis coaching methods. Gallwey's technique is very similar to NLP's modeling, but the process is made simpler because he is present as the perfect model to duplicate. Locating the perfect model to duplicate is the most difficult part of modeling, in my estimation, but if you are willing to expand your search broadly enough, you should succeed.

This brings us back to "The Space Factor." When you restrict your space, you automatically restrict your access to vast resources and a wide range of possible models to emulate. When you remove all restrictions of space and distance, you open yourself up to all of the problem-solving resources of the world, and perhaps beyond.

You Are Your Greatest Resource

When I was a student in Chicago, in the '50s, I had a friend named Burton Philpot Jr., who was a Psychology major at the Illinois Institute of Technology. When I met Burt, he was just in the process of mastering hypnosis and was practicing on anyone he could get to sit in the chair. I was sharing an apartment with a couple of other students. One of them, a farm boy from Iowa, was an excellent hypnotic subject. Under hypnosis, Burt got him to demonstrate a photographic memory and body control which was completely impossible for him in his normal waking state. I have heard stories like the one about a mother who lifted a car off of her pinned child. There have been many feats of super-human strength demonstrated during a crisis. Nevertheless, it was startling to see such a demonstration of hidden strength, perception and recall under hypnosis. It was obvious to me that few people tap even a *small fraction* of their true potential! William James, called the Father of Psychology, wrote back in 1906:

> *Most people live, whether physically, intellectually or morally, in a very restricted circle of their potential being. They make use of a very small portion of their possible consciousness and of their soul's resources in general—much like a man who, out of his whole bodily organism, should get into a habit of using and moving only his little finger. Great emergencies and crises show us how much greater our vital resources are than we had supposed.*

I believe "habit" is the key word here. It supports my earlier comment that *one of the great perpetrators of problems is fixity.* Many of the problems which occur, come about because we settle into *comfortable habit patterns,* and we resist expanding our scope of skills, knowledge and experience. An old proverb says, "iron against iron sharpens the blade." Instead, when challenges come our way we think of them as unwanted problems, rather than opportunities to increase our resources and grow.

Take another look at a problem you are trying to solve. Is there a new skill which would enable you to solve it easily? Consider mastering skills to perform tasks you now pay others to perform for you. If some equipment you own breaks down frequently, could you learn to fix it? Do you pay a large sum annually for someone to do your taxes? If you learned to do them yourself, would you gain more understanding and control over your own finances? Do you trust someone to choose your investments for you? Could you take a class and learn to select your own?

I'm not suggesting it will always be economical to take on these tasks yourself. These are decisions you must make. But it may be a wise investment. Ask yourself how much time you have to invest? How much money? How long would it take to recover that investment? Might you gain new insights which would improve other aspects of your life? If you continually improve your most important resource—your own skills, knowledge and abilities—you will find that you automatically become a more effective problem solver.

Combining Resources

One of the most powerful forces available today is the power of the *laser beam.* The ability of a laser beam to burn through hardened steel is the result of the alignment of frequency and direction of amplified light. A single beam of light has little penetrating power, but when a vast amount of light is gathered, aimed, aligned and concentrated on a single target, the results are awesome. Consider combining the incredible latent power you possess with the incredible latent power of a number of like-minded individuals. Dieters use the "buddy system." Alcoholics go to *Alcoholics, Anonymous* and drug addicts belong to organizations like *Narcotics, Anonymous*. Network and support groups exist for nearly every kind of endeavor or common problem. There are trade associations and clubs within every profession, and it is possible to organize a brain-storming session for just about any problem.

If you don't have to solve it alone, why try to do so?

Use Your Total Resource Power

When problems arise around an apparent lack of money, possessions, time, space or other resources, remember this rule:

Problems are seldom the result of insufficient resources. The needed resources are available if you look long enough and far enough.

PROBLEM SOLVING POWER

CHECKLIST NUMBER TEN

— Utilize Resources—

A Short List for Resolving Financial Resource Problems:

1. Do a thorough inventory of all resources available.

2. List what resources are actually needed to resolve the current problem.

3. Identify any dormant assets that could be liquidated to pay outstanding debts or acquire needed resources. Do so.

4. Identify what resources are being wasted, and what expenses could be trimmed. Determine how unpaid bills might be paid with existing income. Do whatever is necessary to bring these expenses under control.

5. Identify what skills, talents, equipment, and other production capabilities are not being fully used. Utilize these resources more completely for producing income.

6. Set up an expansive training program to greatly increase the production, sales and delivery skills of existing personnel, including yourself.

7. Set up a production-reward system, which effectively motivates your income producers to put out that *extra* effort needed to increase income above outgo in the organization. Remove any penalties for high production.

8. Find an external source of any additional resources needed. Send out a persuasive request for those resources and persist until you get them.

A Short List for Increasing Space Resources:

1. Take a walk around the space or spaces you now possess or can use. Then go around and touch each major object in the space that you possess or can use.

2. Write down what additional space (or spaces) would enable you to solve your problem more easily. Describe it fully. (If possible, go to the space you just described and walk around it, imagining that it is yours for the asking).

3. Write down all of the ways you might gain the use of the desired space. Include purchasing, renting, leasing, sharing and exchanging, plus any others you can think of.

4. Using the *Master Plan Design* in Chapter Nine, create a plan and strategy to obtain (or gain the use of) the space you need to help solve your problem. Be certain your design allows for gradual steps which are achievable at each step along the way.

A Short List for Increasing People Resources:

1. Make a list of all of your present people resources. When the list is complete, note after each person's name, what valuable talent, skill or knowledge that person contributes to you. Also note what you give back in return for that contribution.

2. Make a separate list of the talents, skills or knowledge you could use in people you would choose to assist you in resolving your problem.

3. After each characteristic on the foregoing list, note someone you're aware of who possesses that characteristic. If you know of a specific person whose services you would like to obtain, note that person's name after the appropriate characteristic description. If you don't know anyone who possesses a particular characteristic, write a description of the "ideal" person you might imagine could fill that job.

4. After you have your list of desired people-qualities, along with real or imagined people whose services you would like to have, write what you could offer as pay or as an exchange for those services.

5. Circle every contactable person on your list who has the desired qualities. Also have an exchange to offer which you believe may get that person to work for you or to help you with your project or problem. Start by getting whatever assistance you can with what you have to offer.

6. If you are successful with the foregoing step, you should find you have opened the door to obtaining more helpers. If not, you may have to examine the limitations of what you have to offer, and find a way to make your own resources more valuable so you can attract help more easily.

A List to Find Resources That Are Out of Sight:

1. What resources have been mislaid? Neglected? Hidden? Avoided? Untapped? Unused?

2. What resources have been withheld? Denied? Refused?

3. What resources have been half-used? Unused? Wasted?

4. What could you do to put these resources to work for you?

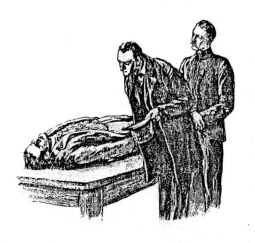

*Physical death is far less painful than the the death of
one's hope that a long-desired dream may be fulfilled.*

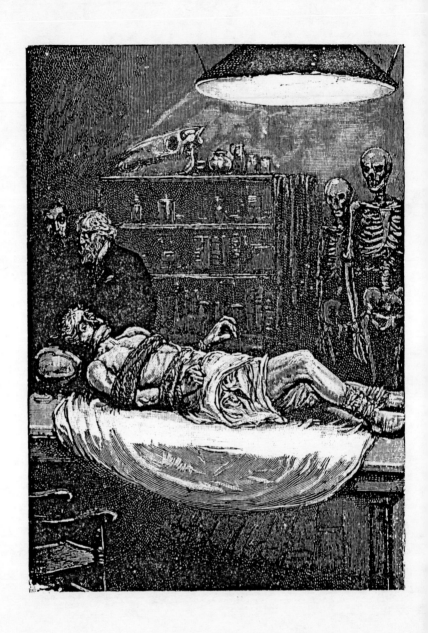

Failing to consider that some of the facts may
have been concealed can keep a problem
persisting.

11. THE POWER OF THE NEGATIVE

"When I go into any business deal, my chief thoughts are on how I'm going to save myself if things go wrong."

J. Paul Getty

Scientists who study the nature of the universe and the powerful forces which move stars and planets and entire galaxies, all marvel at the delicate balance which permits human life on our planet, Earth. If the average temperature was only a hundred degrees higher or lower — trivial by intergalactic standards —human life as we know it couldn't exist. Our physical bodies and the plants and animals on which we depend for survival, all require the delicate balance of air, water, temperature and pressure which makes life possible on this planet.

Balance seems to be a powerful survival force in nature. Some vitamins which are beneficial in proper doses, prove to be detrimental when taken in extreme quantities. Research tests routinely prove that exposing laboratory animals to many substances in extreme quantities produces cancer. "Moderation in all things," counseled Terence, the Roman playwrite. *"Nothing in Excess,"* is engraved on the Temple of Apollo at Delphi, and expressed again by Voltaire: *"Use, do not abuse; neither abstinence nor excess ever renders man happy."* Similar thoughts have been echoed by the Christian apostle Paul, our own Benjamin Franklin, and countless writers since. The two extremes of life, *scarcity* and *excess*, are the basis for many of the problems which we must face every day.

Apparently solving strategies, which work well when applied in moderation, begin to generate more problems when carried to excess. A popular catch-all strategy for problem-solving is "positive thinking," but viewed in the light of critical analysis, positive thinking alone seldom resolves problems. My favorite author on the subject of "luck," Max Gunther, has an entire chapter in his book, *The Luck Factor*, devoted to "The Pessimism Paradox." Gunther quotes Gerald Loeb, one of the "luckiest" men on Wall Street: *"On the stock market optimism can kill you."* And Max reports the counsel of a professional Las Vegas gambler: *"Don't think about winning until you've made yourself ready to lose."* Gunther, who has studied the lives and philosophies of winners in sweepstakes, Las Vegas, the stock market and the business world, concludes that:

> **"The consistently successful executive is emotionally prepared for . . . bad luck and is not demoralized when it strikes. The failure-prone executive, with his twin illusions of immunity and mastery, is likely to be knocked off balance."**

Apparently, as with other forces in the universe, balance is also necessary between optimism and pessimism for effective problem-solving.

Testing: A Vital KEY in the Solving Process

Major problems which many of us face, have to do with a scarcity of, or possible loss of, *money*. For the very poor the problem is how to get some. For much of the middle class the problem is how to get enough to live the good life, while giving as little as possible to the goverment in taxes. For the rich the problem is often how to hold on to what they have, how to invest wisely so they increase rather than decrease their wealth, and also how to minimize the tax bite. Those who are at the level of "How to get enough to survive" assume that when they have climbed a bit up the ladder of success, money will no longer be the major problem. While their anguish over a lack of money may be a daily affair, it is probable that the greatest anguish is experienced by those who have had money and lost it. How much do you imagine is lost to investment scams annually? Stretch your mind to the farthest imaginable extreme. $500 million? A billion? Ten billion? No. Keep going. A June, 1988, *Los Angeles Times* special report on Personal Finance, reported *forty billion dollars* lost annually to investment scams!

The *Times* reports that, "Anything sold has potential for being the basis of a scam: real estate, precious metals, gems and even rock concert tickets, along with vitamins and designer jeans have been the basis for schemes defrauding thousands of hapless investors. Investment fraud can include everything from selling cures for AIDS to rolling back automobile odometers, say the experts. Phony franchises, bogus financial planners and false business billings make regular appearances." Stephen Jones, vice president of law and policy for the Council of Better Business Bureaus says, "Their inventiveness is amazing. As crazy as some of these scams are, people can make them sound very legitimate and they can humiliate you into buying it or badger you into buying it." One deputy district attorney says, "People don't know how to hang up. If they hear a pitch, why not just hang up?"

In a society where TV, radio, magazine and other media ads exaggerate the virtues of every imaginable product, you would think that viewers would develop a healthy cynicism of nearly any sales pitch. Apparently it isn't so when it comes to money. Beautiful brochures and convincing brochures and presentations effectively peddle products which don't exist. Or they leave out important information like a 100% markup or the fact that this incredible scheme could never make money under current market conditions.

Wishful thinking — compulsive optimism — convinces people that the universe owes them more than they have. When a magic opportunity seems to have appeared, they find it *impossible to doubt* that the break they so richly deserve has finally arrived. The sad truth is that a dose of healthy skepticism at this point could save them a great deal of both money and emotional pain.

Testing is the vital link in the problem solving process. The best laid plans of mice and men often do go astray without extensive checking, test runs, test marketing, truth tests and quality tests. In Chapter Six, I stressed the importance of verifying facts and challenging assumptions. Thorough checking of facts alone probably would have saved $20 billion of the $40 billion lost to scams last year.

Quality Checking: A Way to Debug Prospective Solutions

Philip B. Crosby is possibly America's leading quality expert. After serving for fourteen years as corporate vice president of ITT, responsible for worldwide quality operation, he founded his own corporate consulting company which counsels hundreds of companies. Over 15,000 executives have attended his Quality College in Winter Park, Florida. His books, *Quality is Free*, and *The Art of Getting Your Own Sweet Way*, have won international bestselling acclaim. In the June, 1988, issue of *Success* magazine, Crosby stated: "Manufacturing companies spend 25 percent of sales making mistakes; service companies: 40 percent." Think about what these levels of error would mean to you on a personal level. What if you had to spend 25 percent of your paycheck on correcting past mistakes? Or *40 percent!* Crosby's message is: *"Doing it right the first time is not just easier and smarter. It is incredibly profitable!*

Crosby's most recent book, *Quality Without Tears*, provides fourteen steps to what he calls "zero-defects," which could easily eliminate the majority of problems found in most businesses and personal endeavors as well. Throughout this book I have attempted to steer your attention toward thinking of yourself as an organization. I have shown you that there are many "departments" in your world. I hope I have convinced you that you need to define your problem from the viewpoint of each of these departments to arrive at a solution which addresses all dimensions of that problem. In Chapter One of his book, Crosby profiles the *"problem organization."* Let's take a look at Crosby's "problem-company-profile" and see if it applies to your problems on a personal level:

1. Crosby says that in a problem company, the outgoing product

probably *"contains deviations from the published, announced, or agreed-upon requirements."*

When you have designed a tentative solution to your problem, you have to consider the impact of that decision on other people who will be affected by it. If a possible solution is to change your job, how will your family be affected by that change? If a possible solution is to sell your house and move into an apartment, how will making that change affect your children or your spouse? Even changing the furniture in your home or office could disorient people around you. If your solution requires moving to a different city, that could affect friends, club members, contractual commitments, and even your ongoing relationship with your doctor, dentist, attorney and other personal service people.

If you change something without announcing it, you can create far-reaching disturbances. If you announce one kind of change and then *do something else*, major repercussions are nearly guaranteed! When you commit yourself to taking an action which will resolve a problem, you often don't know if your action really will resolve it. To prevent the possibility of multipying your problems if things go wrong, include in your announcement, *what you will do if the tentative solution doesn't work out.* This adds a great deal of predictability for those around you, and will gain you more support for your solving endeavor.

2. Crosby points out that many companies have field service or re-work facilities to *keep customers happy when products don't perform properly.* You've probably been on the receiving end of one of these services. You buy a new appliance, perhaps an air-conditioner. You take it home, plug it in and, right from the start, it doesn't work right. You call the store where you bought it and they direct you to take it to an "authorized service center." At the center they acknowledge that the product doesn't work right, but it is "under warranty" so they will fix it and have it for you in ten days. Theoretically the problem didn't cost you anything, except for the fact that you may have spent several hours trying to operate the unit, trying to find out if you were doing something wrong, calling the store, taking the unit to the service center and finally picking it up. Not only did the problem cost you an enormous amount of time and energy, but it also cost you much in terms of frustration, not to mention the discomfort of doing without the air conditioner for ten days or more after you bought it (usually at the hottest time of the year).

What implication does this have for your solution? The reason you had to go through this ordeal is that *the company had inadequate quality control to begin with!* All they had to do was turn the air conditioner on, the same as you did, to find out it didn't work properly! How does this apply to your problem situation? Why not "turn on" your tentative solution to see if it works? If you have decided to speak to your boss or husband or wife or an employee about a ticklish problem situation, *do a dummy run.* Write out briefly what you intend to say. Anticipate how they will respond and write out how you will deal with their responses in several different ways. Then do a test run. Get a friend to role-play your spouse, boss, employee or other problem person. Make your presentation. Then have your friend feed back the various responses or objections, one at a time, until you can handle them. You will find you handle these responses differently in a real conversation than you do in your mind or on paper. To find out if it works, turn on your "appliance" before you ship it!

3. Crosby says *"Management does not provide a clear performance standard or definition of quality, so the employees each develop their own."* He says that in product companies, getting products out on schedule is the top priority. Next is staying within cost requirements. *The last consideration is the quality of the product!* Naturally sub-standard products will be shipped under these conditions. How does this apply to you? An example might be a time when you are pressed for time or cash. The "solution" you apply at a time like that is likely to be less effective than what you would have chosen if you had *unlimited* time or money.

As a career counselor, I frequently encountered people who were unhappy with their jobs. When contemplating a career change, they were not happy to hear that if they wanted to earn more money, they would have to gain better skills. Getting a better job might mean taking computer training, an accounting course, or a sales and marketing class in the evening, *at their own expense.* It could even mean taking voice or diction coaching, or participating in a public speaking class. Faced with such demanding requirements, many chose a *compromise* solution. Quality considerations vanished. They went for another dead-end job at slightly higher pay. It would be worthwhile to *familiarize* yourself in advance with the *standard of quality* required to solve the problem at hand. Then you would know what you need to improve and you could test the quality of your skills before proceeding.

4. Politicians are famous for "putting their foot in their mouth" and having to "eat their words" (excuse the mixing of metaphors). Their press people then have to spend the next several weeks explaining what the politician "really meant to say." What is the price of such carelessness? Very often the next election. Crosby says that in business *management does not know the price they pay for inconsistency in the quality of their product output.* You will recall he says they spend 25 percent of their product sales dollars and 40 percent of their service dollars doing things wrong or doing them over. He points out that this high cost of correction could easily pay for an incredibly effective *education* and *monitoring* process. And there would be gigantic profits left over! Harold S. Geneen, who managed I.T.& T. for nearly two decades, said, "Quality is not only right, it is free. And it is not only free, it is the most profitable product line we have."

   In the sequence of *recognize, review/revise, familiarize* and *energize*, you have carried out 80 percent of the problem solving process before the *energize* (apply) step. *Familiarize* alone can be such a lengthy process, few people bother to complete it before "energizing" some attempted solution. What will be the consequence of applying an untested solution? Often it will be *repeated* failure! If you have a problem you have been trying to solve for a very long time with no success, you can be sure the reason lies in failing to carry out the *recognize, review/revise,* and *familiarize* steps. An investment in adequate *education and monitoring ability* will pay incredible dividends and guarantee far more effective solutions.

5. Finally Crosby says, *"Management denies that it is the cause of the problem."* Recall earlier in this book when I asked you to imagine you were setting up a simple business. It could have been a lemonade stand, selling girl-scout cookies or cutting lawns. It doesn't matter which one. The process is always the same. As the entrepreneur you would be "Top Management," the *creative source* of the business. As the originator and chief executive of your business, it was your attitude that was seen as representative of your entire business. There is one "trickle-down" phenomenon that you can count on in a business: *If top management is sloppy, indifferent, wasteful or blame-oriented, those attitudes and policies will find their way down to the lowest level of the company, regardless of the stated intent.* As the old saying goes, "your actions speak so loudly I can't hear what you're saying."

In chapter nine, on *Creativity Power,* I introduced you to the idea that often people create their own problems to challenge their survival skills. There is one major benefit which comes from assuming that *if there is a problem, in some way you are creating it.* Anytime something is fully under your control, you can do something about it. But when someone who is not under your control must do what you need to have done, all you can do is try to persuade that person to take action. You are not really in control. You may feel like a person driving a car with someone else's foot on the accelerator. If they start accelerating faster than you can effectively steer the car, you're going to be in for a pretty exciting ride! But if you fully accept *full responsibility* for all aspects of the problem, you may be amazed at how much more in control you feel. Your chance of solving your problem will be multiplied many times!

The Power of the Negative

In our society positive thinking has nearly become a religion. It is certainly true that if you approach a problem you wish to solve with a firm belief that it *can't be solved,* you will have great difficulty finding a solution. But it is also true that if you approach a complex problem which requires special knowledge, training and tools to solve, with nothing but "a positive attitude," you will be in for a great disappointment.

The friends I treasure most are those who are willing to play "Devil's Advocate" for me. When I come up with a bright idea, they are willing to ask me the "hard questions." Have I really thought it through? What will I do if it doesn't work? Is there another approach with less risk? Only your best friends dare ask these questions because they sound more like criticisms than encouragement. Nevertheless I have been grateful that they called my attention to these powerful negative factors *before* I stuck my neck out. That was better than having them let me get stuck in the muck and *then telling me* when it was too late for me to shift gears or change directions. If you have friends who are honest and straightforward and really care what happens to you, be grateful for them.

PROBLEM SOLVING POWER

CHECKLIST NUMBER ELEVEN

(Alternate between answering the positive and the negative question of each pair until you feel a sudden sense of relief or have a new realization. If you suddenly feel the problem is no longer a problem, congratulate yourself and discontinue this checklist.)

In regard to your problem . . . .

P: What problem are you having?
N: What problem are you not having?

P: Where are you?
N: Where are you not?

P: Who are you being?
N: Who are you not being?

P: When did your problem occur?
N: When did your problem not occur?

P: What is happening now?
N: What is not happening now?

P: What sensations have you experienced?
N: What sensations have you not experienced?

P: What have you thought?
N: What have you not thought?

P: What efforts have you made to solve it?
N: What efforts have you not made to solve it?

P: What emotions have you felt?
N: What emotions have you not felt?

P: What have you been willing to look at?
N: What have you not been willing to look at?

P: What have you known for certain?
N: What has been unknown?

P: What new understanding do you now have?

*A problem often reduces to a conflict
of ideas, emotions or intentions.*

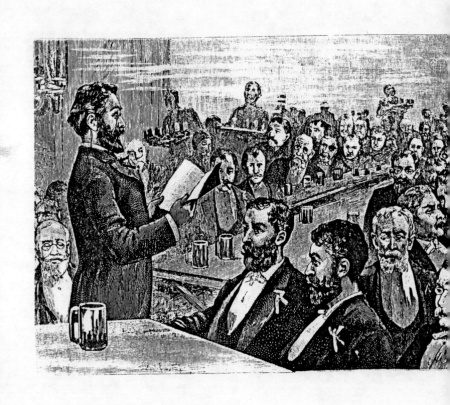

*People are amazingly willing to share
their experience and knowledge.*

12. WILL IT REALLY HELP?
(The ultimate test of an effective solution)

Help: *1. To give assistance to; to aid. 2. To contribute to in some way; to further; promote. 3. To give relief (to those in difficulty or distress); succor. 4. To alleviate or cure.*

Hypothesis: *Any problem can be solved with sufficient help.*

Observation: *Help is really only help if it is considered to be helpful by the person receiving the "help."*

In the *Introduction* to this book, I asked you to consider the departmental breakdown of a business as a basis for all problem solving. I then introduced you to eight common business departments, based on setting up a simple lemonade stand. One of these departments was Public Relations, sometimes called Community Relations. It could be said that this department is the conscience of a business and the department which determines what people think of that business as a citizen in their community. A good PR department helps define a company's values. It strives to establish the company in the eyes of its neighbors as a responsible, caring, contributing entity. Businesses which care about their image contribute *greatly* to the community, through contributions to charities, education and the arts.

The help-oriented activities of a company's public relations or community relations department obviously has a very real problem solving purpose. Even though profit-producing companies ultimately generate most of the income which people obtain through wages (and thus the government obtains through taxes), some people have a feeling that most companies make "obscene" profits. A similar viewpoint contends that most companies destroy the environment and pollute the air and water. Some people even believe that most companies do more harm than good, somehow ignoring the fact that without the existence of companies to pay wages, few communities would exist at all!

Whether these viewpoints are justified or not, companies must attempt to counteract hostile opinions because the public is the buyer of most products produced. A bad PR image could result in a loss of sales and, therefore, lower profits. Contributing to the community helps a company counteract any negative image. The company hopes these measures will make people more willing to buy their products. You might consider this a very cynical view of "help" and tend to think most corporate PR efforts are insincere. Whether true or not, the fact is that corporate contributions are a major factor in keeping many charities and public service projects alive. The value of that help can't be belittled. To solve problems effectively the help factor must be considered. This is just as true for you as for corporations, states and even nations.

HELP--What Is It?

"Help" may be one of the strangest activities of which Mankind is capable. Other animal species instinctively cooperate for mutual survival in varying ways, but among animals lower than Man, this cooperation tends to be consistent within each species. Man is nearly unique in his varied reactions to the idea of "help."

Some people crave help and won't make a move without it. Others are living examples of the phrase: "Please Mother! I'd rather do it myself!" These individuals wear the equivalent of a sign which says "No Help Wanted." When it comes to solving problems or, more importantly, becoming an effective problem solver, both of these extreme positions on the subject of "help" will stand in the way.

From my own observations over the past half-century, I have come to believe that the desire to help, to contribute, is almost instinctive in the developing human child. Children already begin to reach out and attempt to help and contribute in infancy, if only by smiling to entertain. If a child's parent is perceptive and cognizant of the importance of nurturing this trait, that parent will encourage the child's earlist efforts, no matter how clumsy, and build that innate sense of responsibility. These are the beginnings of the urge to accept the challenges of the species—to become a *problem-solver* for the human race. It's part of the evolutionary urge within us all.

How We Lose the Urge to Help

Earlier I spoke about the survival instinct of various animal species. Each species is endowed with some major survival characteristic. The animal kingdom breaks down into the hunters and the hunted. Among the hunters the main survival characteristics are fighting tools: the claws of the cat and the fangs of the dog and the wolf. Among these species it is instinctive to exercise these fighting tools to keep practiced for times of crisis, to attack or defend. Even your pet cat claws at your sofa or your drapes or a scratching post, and your dog chews bones or your shoes to keep sharp. The urge is built-in by Mother Nature.

Man, as a species, is a hunter too, and he is endowed with the most powerful tool of all, which has allowed him to become the master of all of the animal kingdom. That is, of course, his brain, his mind, his problem-solving ability. Like the lower animals, he too practices daily to keep his tool sharp for times of crisis, to attack or defend. How does he do this? He seeks out problems to solve, and if there are none, *he creates them!* In Chapter Nine I asked you: "Have you ever created a problem for yourself?" The answer, of course, was "yes." We all have, many times, and rightfully so. We must practice solving problems constantly to keep our minds sharp and to ensure our long-term survival. Apparently it's instinctive!

Nations go through about the same stages of existence as the human organism. First there is the "birth" of a nation, then a period of struggle to learn "to walk," and then a period of intense effort and productivity to become mature and strong. When this is accomplished there is a leveling off and a long period of relative stability, similar to adulthood, with random up and down cycles.

We have to turn to history to view the final stages of great nations. In a model like the Roman Empire, we can see the stages of gradual decline and final destruction. These final stages are not unlike those of the senior citizen who retires from productive life, weakens, and finally dies. Fortunately, in the case of a nation or an individual, *it doesn't have to happen!* All senior citizens don't retire from a productive life, accept an existence of perpetual leisure and wait to die. Many renew themselves daily and extend their lives incredibly, by continual productive involvement. But that takes motivation, determination and a real commitment to *living* and contributing! It is also the KEY to reversing the decline and enhancing the revitalization of a nation!

So how, you are probably asking, does this relate to "helping" and developing problem solving ability? Unfortunately it is possible to *over-ride* the natural instinct to sharpen survival skills. When we domesticate dogs and cats, we punish them for scratching and chewing on our possessions, and we provide abundant food so that there is no real need to struggle for survival. By taking a pet, we automatically make a life-long commitment to *completely* care for that animal's needs until it dies. Eventually it learns to prefer comfort to challenge and so suppresses its instinctive hunting skills.

In the human it is also possible to override the instinct to seek out problems and challenges to sharpen the wit. By supplying every need for a developing adult, by solving every problem for a child, or by dulling the urge for challenge in any individual by enforcing a constant diet of amusement, comfort and sensual pleasures, one can turn a dynamic, potentially productive human being into a useless vegetable. This is carrying "help" to its ultimate, destructive extreme.

The same result can also be accomplished by a *denial of opportunity* to produce, help, or contribute. Once reduced to no more than a seeker of sensual gratification, a young person's attraction to drugs is inevitable in our world of ready access. I've seen it happen over and over again, in varying degrees. On a grand scale it can become the road to national ruin.

The Decline from "Helpful" to "Helpless"

A friend of mine married a lady who already had a son. The boy's father saw the boy regularly and, because he was wealthy, he doted on the kid and provided for his every need and desire. Every time the kid would think of something he would like to work and save for, the father bought it for him before he could lift finger one. Gradually the kid, who was naturally ambitious and productive, became fixated on comfort and self-indulgence. By the age of 21, he had dropped out of college several times, and used drugs to suppress any urge to produce. Nevertheless his father still supported him and continued to try to solve his every problem. Statistics show that today, in the U.S., a large percentage of kids still live at home in their late twenties, and the use of drugs by unemployed youths (and unhappily employed youths) has become legendary.

Ben, another friend of mine, has been a manager of a fast-food restaurant for nearly twenty years. He has won countless awards for top efficiency and production, and has often produced nearly double the profit of the next highest producing store in his chain. He has accomplished this feat by having an incredible talent for spotting motivated kids and training them to function well in a short period of time. Over the years he has set records for low turnover in an industry where employee turnover is known to be a revolving-door situation. In the past year, Ben tells me that it has become all but impossible to find motivated kids, or kids that are not on drugs. He says that kids from the affluent neighborhoods won't work if they don't have to. The ones who will work these days can't keep straight (off drugs), for more than a couple of weeks before they fall apart. Two teachers I know tell me that today their classes are 90% filled with unmotivated vegetables or undisciplined rowdies, and the school system has taken away all of the disciplinary measures they were once free to use.

How has this state of affairs come about? In Rome, affluence led to decadence. Slaves did the work and the children of the affluent grew up in unchallenged comfort and self-indulgence. A similar state of affairs exists in many parts of the U.S. today, even though that affluence is more and more an illusion supported by a huge national debt, addictive consumer credit, and over-consumption of goods produced in all over the world. The result of this illusory affluence is a large population of relatively prosperous parents producing less and less productive offspring. This same so-called "affluence" has brought about an unspoken ideal in America: a perception that the highest good, the greatest value, is a comfortable, easy, self-gratifying, problem-free (and thus challenge-free), existence. TV, films, magazines and ads all shout out the same message: "The best life is a life of easy riches, endless leisure, perpetual entertainment, expensive houses, cars, clothes, lovers and abundant food, drink and (by implication) drugs."

What can be done about this?

Changing Problem People into Solvers

It is only necessary to provide opportunity and challenge on an achievable gradient to build strong, contributing youths, employees or citizens. Productivity has continually declined in the older, developed nations of the West, as these nations focused more and more on comfort and womb-to-tomb security. These nations have become soft "senior citizens" looking for lives of endless leisure. As I write this, the big producers are those in the East who are in the growth stages of development. There, *opportunity* is most highly valued, and productivity is most highly rewarded, even though at a much lower (and thus more challenging) rate than here in the West. Challenge, and a determination to meet that challenge, has continually made Japan, Taiwan, Korea, Singapore and Hong Kong stronger. Even the Chinese are jumping on that band wagon. What kind of real *help* can society provide here in the West to improve our ability to compete?

Two Suggested Solutions That Might Help

To compete in the West it seems to me that we need to do two things:

First, it is beginning to appear that we must legalize "recreational" drugs and put them under government control just as we do alcohol and tobacco. In that way we can deny the criminals and drug runners their ill-gotten profits and fatten our government coffers by taxing these controlled commodities.

Second, and even more important, to solve the youth unemployment problem, we need to *popularize productivity, responsibility and challenge*. This is a far more difficult task because we would have to turn around a trend toward comfort-seeking which has been accelerating for twenty years. John F. Kennedy tried to reverse that trend with his famous motto: "Ask not what your country can do for you, but what you can do for your country." He knew that when one feels able to help and contribute, self-confidence, self-respect and self-reliance will also develop faster. His efforts in promoting a Peace Corps and trying to develop something like a Jobs Corps were efforts in the right direction. I believe that 18 months of National Service for every youth is an absolute *must!* There should be a "Corps" for every branch of government, including a "Justice Corps" for aspiring legal students, an "Agricultural Corps" for those who are inclined in that direction, and a "Transportation Corps" as well as an expanded "Conservation Corps" and "Peace Corps" or "Foreign Service Corps." To become good citizens and producers kids need an opportunity to get a closer look at the government, the nation and the world, and most of all they need to get away from their parents and their peer groups long enough to establish their own identity and gain some confidence in their own ability to be productive and to contribute broadly. An approach of this sort would be *real* help!

What can you do about it within your own sphere of life?

On a more personal level those of you who are parents, teachers or employers, must recognize that you are never doing a favor for kids or people by over-helping and *solving their problems for them.* When you rob people of their challenges, you are robbing them of their opportunity to grow and become stronger and more independent. In the long run you are crippling them. When a child expresses those early desires to "help," it is vital that you apply some ingenuity and figure out a way to permit that "help." If you love your family, you will do all you can to make it strong. If you love your country you will do the same. We should prove that an affluent society does not also have to be a decadent society!

Asking for Help When You Need It

Up until now I have asked you to think about the consequences for people who have been *overhelped* and inadvertently taught to expect unqualified help at all times, thus avoiding the necessity of taking on any personal challenge. Now take a look at the other extreme: the compulsively "macho" personality who refuses help and insists on solving every problem alone. In the long run, this person is also doomed to failure in a world as complex as ours. Ours is a society built upon cooperative effort. Not one of our towering buildings could have been built by a single individual. Our roads, our bridges, our water and power utilities and most means of transportation (other than walking and horse-back riding) depend upon the cooperative efforts of a great many people to bring them into existence. Our entire society is built on a foundation of mutual *help*.

What all of this is leading up to, is the observation that:

> *A person's effectiveness as a problem-solver often depends on the ability to discover and enlist the aid of other individuals who are most able to help resolve the problems at hand.*

If you are having problems with your automobile, unless you are a professional mechanic, how fast you solve your car problem depends directly on how fast you find a mechanic who can fix it. If you are having physical problems with your body, your speed of solution will depend on how quickly you can find one or more medical practitioners who can effectively treat your condition. These situations, of course, are rather obvious, but many other problem situations are not so obvious.

When it comes to seeking help, there is always the question of ability to pay. Doctor bills and lawyer bills are at the top of the list for the most expensive personal services available in the U.S. When you have an emotional problem with a boyfriend or girlfriend or husband or wife, you may not immediately think of going to a psychologist or other psychotherapist because of the expense involved. Nevertheless, in the long run it is always more costly to attempt to solve a complex problem by "trial and error" than to call upon the incredible level of professional know-how which is available in our day. The are more people who are struggling to achieve financial security than there are those who have already achieved it, and yet the brilliant financial advisors who are available are mainly sought out by those who already have achieved relative financial security. Those who need the help the most, rarely ask for it and so they continue to struggle.

The willingness of most people to help in time of need is amazing. To obtain effective help, however, it may be necessary to offer something in exchange, if only love or appreciation.

An Expert's Advice on Asking for Help

There is one man who has eloquently addressed the issue of asking for the help that many people (and perhaps you) cannot afford to buy. Every week syndicated columnist and self-made millionaire Percy Ross gives away thousands of dollars in gifts and money through his nationally acclaimed column, "Thanks a Million." Ross has been likened to an Ann Landers who goes beyond just giving advice, to also giving the *wherewithal* to follow that advice in many instances!

He receives over 5,000 letters every week, generally asking for money, and he grants the wishes of many of the writers. When does he say "yes" and when does he say "no?" In his book *Ask for the Moon and Get It*, Percy tells us that he decides on the basis of *how the person asks!* Percy provides a ten-point checklist in his book, which gives the specifics of who, what, why, when, where and how to ask for the help you need, without manipulating people. While reading his book, I was struck once again by the parallels to the *stages of growth*, the *phases of problem-solving*, and the eight divisions of an ideal organization:

Recognize: Percy says you must *recognize* what it is that you really need or want before you can ask for it. At you have read through this book, you have had many opportunities to define your problems and your needs. Apparently Percy and I agree that this step is always the first essential one.

Review/Revise: He tells us we must overcome our inner barriers to asking. Very often this can require searching one's soul and *reviewing* the past to find the basis for one's *fear* of asking, to find the conditioning that one should be "too proud to ask," or the idea that one is "too insignificant to deserve to ask." Percy suggests taking a *direct approach to revising* these reluctances to asking by simply "gritting your teeth" and pushing through your own resistance. If this is too difficult, he suggests trying something like a "buddy system," where you find someone to talk to, who you can count on to encourage you to gradually break through your barriers and to reach out for the help you need.

Familiarize: Even when simply asking for help to resolve a problem, you need to know who to ask. Then you need to present "a good case," as Percy puts it, for receiving what you need. There is no substitute for doing your home work: finding out who can best provide you with what you need, and then finding out what kind of request that person or organization will respond to.

Energize: Once you've done your homework, you are ready to ask. Percy says *how you ask* is what determines whether or not he (or anyone else) will honor your request. The anecdotes and stories he presents in his book to illustrate the power of the art of asking are so vivid, I wouldn't attempt to convey them here. What I will pass along, however, are four rules which he rightfully emphasizes above all: *(1) Ask artfully, (2) Request or invite, (3) Don't demand or beg,* and *(3) Show respect.* These may seem obvious, but Percy indicates that many requests are denied for the lack of these simple elements of good taste in asking.

Organize: Like the motivational speaker who tells us that "ninety percent of failures come from quitting," Percy advises us to "ask and keep asking." If one is seeking help to reach a truly important goal in life, it is worth pursuing with dogged persistence. Percy tells us to be creative in asking. He tells a revealing story of his own success when he lost his fur business and became "flat broke." He was a professional auctioneer and he approached a contractor who wanted to auction off $100,000 of heavy equipment. Percy wanted a standard ten or fifteen percent for the auctioning job, but the man would only pay five percent. Percy says he really needed the money but felt he couldn't afford to do the job for so little. Then he says, "I was "half-way home when an inspiration hit me. I could approach the situation from a different angle." It had occured to him that if he could find enough other sellers of heavy equipment to raise the overall merchandise value from $100,000 to over a million dollars, then the five percent commission on the auction would meet his financial needs. He tells us that this approach was so successful, he not only solved this one-time problem, but found a new business which put him back on the road to becoming a millionaire over the next eight years. Organizing an "asking campaign" can require trying many different creative approaches.

Utilize: Percy notes that whenever you ask for something, you're not really approaching the bargaining table empty handed. You always have something to give in return. It may be an opportunity to share in the profits of a joint venture, a better return on an investment, more conscientious effort on your part for a raise, or just appreciation, understanding and credit for the giving a gift. My friend Ed Morler, who presents negotiation skill seminars for many of the largest investment banking firms in the U.S., says that one key to effective negotiation is to realize that very often the other party in a negotiation *values something that you have to offer far more than you realize.* You may be focusing totally on money when the other guy mainly wants something that you can easily and inexpensively provide, like information, access rights, screen credits or press recognition which costs you nothing. The key, he says, is to *probe* to find out what the other guy wants, and then *inspect your own resources!* You may find that you have far more to give in return than you had realized.

Capitalize: Hesiod, a Greek poet who scholars believe was a comtemporay of Homer's, wrote some of the world's first "didactic" poetry (that is poetry meant to be instructive rather than entertaining). In his famous poem, *Works and Days,* he says, "*right timing is in all things the most important factor.*" Later, from around the year 1600, we find this famous quote from Shakespeare's play, Julius Caesar, "*There is a tide in the affairs of men, which taken at the flood, leads on to fortune.*" It has long been recognized that it is vital to *capitalize* on opportunities which present themselves at *precisely the right time.* There is generally a time to ask for help which will be more likely to bear fruit than any other time. Children seem to instinctively sense these times in their parents, and unerringly ask for and get things they want when their parents are most succeptable. How does one know when to ask? It may be time to return to the *familiarize* step and learn more about your prospective benefactor.

Another of my favorite authors is Robert Conklin, who, in his book *How to Get People to Do Things,* effectively focuses in on the basics of persuading, selling, motivating, guiding and relating to others. Conklin tells a story about a time the mother of multi-millionaire Marshall Field gave the University of Chicago one million dollars. A director of nearby Northwestern University inquired why a similar grant was not made to their institution. Mrs. Field simply replied, "Northwestern never asked me." Robert likes to emphasize that *people do things for their reasons, not for your reasons.* Perhaps his favorite story is about the time Michael Faraday, the inventor of the electric motor, approached Wil-

- 158 -

liam Gladstone, the British Prime Minister, for the statesman's endorsement. "What good is it?" Gladstone inquired. "Someday you will be able to *tax* it," replied Faraday, thereby instantly winning Gladstone's approval. He recognized Gladstone's motivation and *capitalized* on it to achieve his own objective.

Maximize: Percy Ross's final rule is "Go beyond *me* to *we!*" He says that a KEY point in his decision to honor or refuse a request is whether or not the inquirer is seeking to benefit a broader range of people than himself or herself. Requests which offer to return something to the giver, or to provide help to parents, family, the handicapped or underprivileged are given priority. "Maximize" means *To make as great as possible.* The idea of the *ideal solution* was put forth in 1720 in Francis Hutcheson's "Inquiry Concerning Moral Good and Evil." He concluded, "That action is best which procures the greatest happiness for the greatest numbers."

Using the Magic of "HELP" To Solve People Problems

The real magic in human relationships is achieved through the bond of mutual help. The need for help and the ability to give help keeps people communicating and exchanging help even though they may have radically different viewpoints, purposes and frames of reference. The surest way to establish communication (with a relatively sane individual) is to:

>   *1. Offer to help.*
>   *2. Ask for help.*
>   *3. Accept help when offered.*
>   *4. Acknowledge help when received.*
>   *5. Offer an exchange of help when possible.*

Of all of the eight elements in the *octagon*, the one which is most effective for giving problem-solving help is *communication.* Obviously it is true that people often need other elements: Resources, knowledge, creativity and productive effort can be extremely helpful when needed, but the easiest to give and often the most valuable to receive is *communication.*

Entire volumes have been written on the subject of how to help through communication, but there is one procedure that I have observed to always be effective. Mothers seem to instinctively help upset children by listening in the following manner:

1. *They usually make physical contact, holding a small child in their arms or their lap. They may just hold an older child's hand, or give them a hug before listening.*

2. *After encouraging a child to "tell me all about it," they sit quietly and listen, usually without interrupting except to ask for a little clarification.*

3. *They will encourage the child to keep talking until the entire story has been related, but as soon as the upset seems to be gone and a smile appears, the child is sent on his or her way.*

While it may not always be practical to make or sustain physical contact while listening (although I think it would be preferable even with adults), this simple approach to giving help through communication is perhaps Man's most effective tool for helping. I can think of very few instances in which this kind of help is not appropriate.

Before you rush off to get involved in "helping," however, it would be wise to assess your own views on "help." Note: *(1) Kinds of help you enjoy giving; (2) Kinds of help you enjoy receiving; (3) Kinds of help you resent having to give; (4) Kinds of "help" you resent having thrust upon you.* Once you are certain exactly what help means to you and what you can do to *really* help others solve their problems, you may be ready to venture into the world of helping and being helped—a much trickier world than most would ever imagine.

PROBLEM SOLVING POWER

<u>C H E C K L I S T   N U M B E R   1 2</u>

Check your asking and helping power:

Recognize: Have you *recognized* what it is that you really need or want?

Review/Revise: Have you overcome your inner barriers to asking? If not, have you searched your "soul" and *reviewed* the past to find any reason for: (1) A fear of asking? (2) A feeling that you should be "too proud to ask?" or (3) An idea that you are "too insignificant to deserve to ask?" Or have you tried finding a "buddy" who you can count on to encourage you to gradually break through your barriers and to reach out for any help you need?

Familiarize: Have you found out who can best provide you with what you need, and what kind of request that person or organization will respond to?
The need for help and the ability to give help keeps people communicating and exchanging help even though they may have radically different viewpoints. To establish communication, have you: (1) Offered to help? (2) Asked for help? (3) Accepted help when offered? (4) Acknowledged help when received? (5) Offered an exchange of help when possible?

Energize: Now that you know who to ask, have you worked out: How to ask artfully? How to request or invite rather than demand or beg? How to show respect? How to present a good case that is likely to obtain what you are asking for? Exactly how to make your strong initial presentation or request?

Organize: Have you organized a sustained effort to "ask and keep asking?" Do you have a strategy to help you maintain dogged persistence? Have you organized an "asking campaign" utilizing many different creative approaches?

Utilize: You're never really approaching the bargaining table empty handed. You always have something to give in return. Have you itemized what you have to offer in exchange for what you need? Have you worked out a strategy to *probe* to find out what the other guy wants? To offer it?

Capitalize: It is vital to *capitalize* on opportunities which present themselves at *precisely the right time*. How do you know when to ask? It may be time to return to the *familiarize* step. How might you learn more about your prospective benefactor? People do things for *their* reasons, not for your reasons. What reason might your prospect have to honor your request?

Maximize: Percy Ross's final rule is "Go beyond *me* to *we!* He says that a KEY point in his decision to honor or refuse a request is whether or not the inquirer is seeking to benefit a broader range of people than himself or herself if the wish is granted. How will what you request benefit others?

*People are sometimes reluctant to offer or to ask
for help because of strong emotional feelings.*

For centuries men and women used brawn and brute
force to solve problems and shape their world.
Today the rule is: "Work smarter rather than harder."

13. PRODUCTIVITY AND FLOW POWER

Produce! Produce! Were it but the pitifullest, infinitesimal fraction of a product, produce it in God's name! 'Tis the utmost thou hast in thee? Out with it then!
—*Thomas Carlyle (1795-1881)*

The dictionary defines "flow" as: *To move or run freely in the manner characteristic of a fluid."* In speaking about the human body, *to flow is to live!* When the blood stops flowing, or the digestive juices and lymph flows stop supplying nutrients to vital body parts, the body dies. When the flows don't completely stop, but only slow up, the degree of aliveness and health of the body declines too. The health of the body is determined largely by how fast the various fluids keep flowing. Motion and *flow* is the major evidence of life!

The word "flow" has also found its way into other areas of life, completely unrelated to fluids. In business we speak of product flow, or merchandise flow, or "cash flow." Regardless of where we encounter the word, we always think of something *moving or running freely.* When a river bed dries up, there is no longer any water flow. When our income sources dry up, we speak of having a "cash flow problem." It follows, therefore, that you could have a "sales flow problem," a "personnel flow problem," a "creative idea flow problem," or a "love relationship flow problem."

When a flow *slows up,* it usually creates a problem, but the worst problem is a total STOP! (Notice that even the *word* brings you to a halt!) Along with most of us who drive cars, you have probably experienced the "Great American Nightmare." You are in heavy traffic on a stiflingly hot day when the traffic *flow* comes to a complete STOP! To make matters even worse, you are on a bridge or freeway or in a tunnel and there is no exit in sight. All you can do is sit there. If the equivalent of this happened to the flow of blood flow in your blood stream, you would be history in minutes!

The most frustrating problems which tie up our time and attention are problems which are *totally stopping* a forward flow of one sort or another. At a time like this, you *really* need an arsenal of problem solving weapons to help you blast your way out of that traffic jam, that log-jam—*that very fixed, stopped, stuck situation*—which is preventing your forward flow and aliveness.

Over the years, I have gone to great lengths to analyze these "stopped points" when they occur. I've tried every solving strategy people have suggested or written about, and many that I dreamed up myself. Some strategies work nearly every time, at least partially, so that you can begin to get "unstuck." When you're totally stopped, even a little forward movement helps a lot. Here are some of the strategies I have collected which I (and many other people) have found to be effective:

Uncertainty: The Great Stopper!

A definite "NO" is better than a "maybe." You may not immediately agree with that statement. There was a time when I didn't believe it either. Chauvenist males used to brag that when a girl said "no," she meant "maybe," and when she said "maybe" she meant "yes," therefore when she said "no," she really meant "yes." I have found that "maybe" never means "yes" — not in personal relationships, nor social, nor business relationships. What it does mean is, "Sit there and wait. I haven't made up my mind yet." So where does that leave you or me? It leaves us *stopped* until that "maybe" becomes either a "no" or a "yes."

Have you found yourself stopped on a project because you were waiting for someone else's decision? Or have you found you were not moving on to a *new* job, project, sale, or activity because you were still waiting for some "yes" or "no" answer regarding the old one? When I first worked in sales I found that I was reluctant to press sales prospects for a "yes" or "no" answer, because I was unwilling to have them say "no." Unfortunately some people will say "maybe" forever, rather than admitting they will probably never buy your product—or your idea or your proposal—or anything else from you. If you allow that "maybe" to tie up your time and attention, you have stuck yourself with an unnecessary stop or loss. It's better to get a definite "NO" than a "maybe." At least then you can shift over to some other activity or project where there is a *real* chance that you will get a "yes!"

Spotting the "Pivotal Point"

Waiting for a "maybe" to become a "yes" isn't the only way uncertainty is the Great Stopper. Another classic *stop* is the old "fork in the road" routine. You're driving along, following directions to a friend's house. You haven't been there before, so you've got this scrap of paper with your friend's directions written on it. As you drive along on a major street described in his directions, suddenly you come to this *fork* in the road that he didn't mention! Do you take the right fork or the left fork? He didn't tell you. What do you do now? You are forced to ask someone, to call him up, or to stop at a gas station to get directions or a map. Faced with an unexpected choice, you were *uncertain* of which way to go. You were *stopped* until you found the answer.

In most life situations we are faced with more than two choices. Most junctures in life are more like six-way intersections, with no street signs or markers to show the way. These are problems like: "What job to take?" "What college to go to?" "Who to date and who not to?" "Where to invest my money?" "Where to put my next sales effort?" "Who to hire, who to fire and who to keep?" Decisions like these face us with an almost infinite number of choices. How to choose? Where do you begin? *To not decide leaves you completely stopped,* standing still at the intersection like the driver facing an unexpected fork in the road.

The best rule I have found is:

Recognize the principal pivotal point
on which further progress depends.

In choosing a job, or school, or client, or even a lover, there is usually a KEY factor which will ultimately decide which way you will go. If you are stopped or uncertain, it is usually because you have not *recognized* what that KEY pivotal factor is. To isolate that KEY requirement, a useful practice is to write down what choices you would *absolutely NOT* accept. What jobs wouldn't you accept? Why not? What schools would you definitely not go to? Why not? What kind of client would you definitely not serve or sell to? Why not? What kind of person would you definitely not have as a lover? Why not? As you go through this process, you may soon recognize what you really want. Certainty may replace uncertainty. Then the choice will become obvious and simple.

Take Time to Look and Think

When you're caught up in the need to solve a critical problem, *time* is usually a big factor. Money must be obtained by a certain date. A job, project, or school paper must be finished by a certain time. There is a deadline which you must meet. The time element multiplies the pressure on you solve the problem. The last thing you might consider doing is *taking time out* to sit down and write out what's happening—stating what your options are at this point —or what alternative events might occur, depending on what you decide or do. Nevertheless, this is *exactly* what you should do to speed things up! Does that sound ridiculous? It's not. Here's why.

Let's go back to driving on the road again. This time you have a map and you're driving along toward a new destination.

When you started out you had a general idea of where you were going, but now that you're almost there, you need to focus in on specific exits and street names. You're on a freeway, so you can't read the map while you're driving, but you're late for your appointment and you feel you can't afford to stop. You decide to take your chances and *guess* which exit you should take. You go five miles further and exit, but the exit you choose is wrong. Now you take the time to look at the map. The exit you wanted was five miles back. If you had stopped to look at the map then, you would have saved the ten or fifteen minutes it took you to drive the extra ten miles. Get the idea?

When you're not sure of where you're going, it's *always economical to take the time to park and look at the possibilities*. Stop and draw yourself a map of where you're going with your project, or your job, or your relationship. Use something like the problem solving tools in this book to evaluate your situation, before flying blind any further. It's well worth the time!

Tracing the Flow: The Heavy-Duty Approach

Probably the *most* frustrating problem is the one that seems completely *unsolvable*. No matter what you do, you can't seem to change the situation. Perhaps it is a financial problem, like poor sales in business, or a personnel problem of not being able to find the right person for the project or job. It may be an overall problem of not being able to balance a budget. No matter what you do, you can't seem to catch up. I'm certain you have had some such problem which seemed "unsolvable." The common characteristic of such a problem is its apparent *permanence*. After you have tried everything you can think of, *where do you now direct your efforts?*

To approach this kind of problem, we have to turn our attention back to the world of physics and fluid dynamics. The KEY word, as we have found, is "flow". Remember, the dictionary defines "flow" as: *To move or run freely in the manner characteristic of a fluid*." We noted that the word "flow" had found its way into other areas of life completely unrelated to fluids, like "cash flow" or "production flow." Regardless of where we encounter the word, we always think of something *moving or running freely*. The "unsolvable" problem occurs when the cash flow, the communication flow, the merchandise flow, or the love flow STOPS completely. When all efforts to get things flowing again seem to utterly fail, what can be done about a problem of this sort?

I have found one of the most effective approaches to be what I call the "plumbing solution." Plumbers always deal with fluid flow problems. Luckily for them, the fluid is always flowing in pipes and it's easy to trace the problem in the pipes. The first thing a plumber does is to trace back along the pipes to the *source* of the fluid flow. This is usually a main pipe line coming in from the city water supply. There is a main faucet which completely turns off the flow from that water supply. By going back to the point where the water flow originates, he can tell right away if water is flowing into the system. Similarly one could trace back up a dry river bed, to find out where the flow had stopped: Had the water simply been dammed up or diverted at some point, or was the origin point of the water flow high up in the mountains completely dried up? Tracing the flow back to its point of origin immediately reveals this vital information.

Analyze the Flow

To resolve a flow problem in your business, career, or life in general, you need to do a similar analysis. Take out a piece of paper. Draw a long line which represents "the flow." Then write some dates on that line. If possible, write the earliest date the flow began, at the very beginning of the line. This could be when you first started in business or on a job or on a project. Next note the *last date* that the activity was "flowing" satisfactorily. Finally note when you *first noticed* the flow had stopped, or nearly stopped. This is very much like the plumber tracing back to points along the pipe where the water is still flowing, until he comes to a point where the water is no longer flowing (or not flowing well). He knows there is some *obstruction* in the pipe at that point. And he can now be certain it will be productive to *totally direct his efforts* toward repairing that section of pipe. How would you like to be that certain of the action needed to resolve one of your problems?

Once we leave the very obvious and tangible world of water pipes, the task of identifying a stopped flow point and getting that flow to resume becomes much more difficult. Perhaps a couple of examples will point you in the right direction, but circumstances can be very different for each person's problem. First let's look at the world of computers. In the computer world, nearly every operator has had a particularly exasperating experience called *computer lock-up*. This can occur when the computer has been given a command it *cannot carry out*. No alternative response has been programmed in, like a message which says, "Invalid command—please try another." Computers are very "smart", but simultaneously very "stupid." Most can only carry out one command at a time, and then only if it is on a pre-programmed track. Nothing else will work.

People are far more versatile than most computers. A person can on several "commands" or projects at one time. But when a person runs into a total "STOP" in some direction, he or she will move just like the computer. If there seems to be no alternative, the person will experience a "lock-up" phenomena similar to that found in the computer.

The main characteristic of *lock-up*, whether on the computer or in your daily life, is the *sheer frustration* of it. The computer just sits there and blinks at you. No matter what key you press, nothing moves, nothing changes. It is just simply *stuck!"* Fortunately you have the option of turning the computer off and starting over, although this usually means you will lose whatever data you had been working on when it locked up. In life such an option is seldom available. You can't just switch off your business or your job or your marriage without major repercussions and changes in your life. So you may feel forced to leave the "locked-up" problem sitting there, like the computer, blinking at you, until you accept the necessity of making a major change or you find some acceptable alternative.

Using Your Analysis to Unblock the Flow

How do you translate the plumbers approach to finding an obstruction in a pipe into finding an obstruction in your sales flow, cash flow, work flow or other problem flow? First go back to the line you drew on your paper to represent the flow. Look at the point where it seems like the flow stopped. Then look back at what happened a little earlier than that point. You'll usually find that something *confusing* happened there. Remember, the dictionary defines a problem as *a question or situation that presents uncertainty, perplexity or difficulty.* "Perplexity" means *confused, puzzled or bewildered.* One of the most useful of all problem-solving principles is:

Confusions can be eliminated by identifying
exactly what, when, where, why and how.

Let's take another driving example. Recall a time when you were driving to a new destination. Assume you were "flowing" along the highway just fine until you reached the place where you were supposed to turn off. Let's imagine you were looking for a sign that said "Breckenridge Road West" just before you came to the next town. Suddenly you noticed you had come to the town. You had been watching very closely but did not see a sign that said "Breckenridge Road West." Your flow stopped. You became confused. You were looking for a sign that never appeared, and that left

- 170 -

you bewildered. You didn't know which way to go.. ~~puter~~ which was given a command it couldn't carry ou~~,~~ left sitting and blinking.

In real life you would probably get on the freeway ~~,~~ back the way you came, to see if you could find the exit were looking for. After you had driven back a mile or two, suddenly you might see the "Breckenridge Road West" sign and turn off. Imagine that as you turn, you look across to the other side and notice that there is no turn-off on the other side. The directions you had been given assumed that you would be coming from the opposite direction, but just like the plumber tracing back on the pipe, you traced back until you found the right turn off.

The first time I noticed this phenomena was when I was studying algebra. I would be working along comfortable on an assignment of a group of problems, when suddenly I would encounter one which totally confused me. I would then back-track through the text book or go over my notes on the professor's lecture, until I found some more information about the type of problem. I had failed to understand. When I located the earlier instructions and studied them until I understood them, I was able to solve the confusing problem and continue *flowing* along on completing my assignment. You may have experienced the same thing in high school or college.

The tricky part about this problem solving technique is (1) correctly *identifying the confusion,* and (2) tracing back to discover *where you should direct your efforts to clear up that confusion.* Once you have gotten that far, it's time to *define terms* and *separate out facts from assumptions and opinions.* You will need the skills you began to develop in chapter six, *Knowledge Power.* If you are able to do that effectively, you should be able to get things flowing again in record time.

Focused "Productivity" vs. Effort and Force

Production statistic: *The number of products of acceptable quality completed per unit of time.*

Hypothesis: *Any problem can be solved with sufficient productive action.*

If you look back over the preceding chapters, you will see that we have looked at *knowledge* as the KEY to sorting out effective solutions. We have looked at *communication* as a universal solvent. We have considered *creativity* to be the ultimate solving tool,

.. used without undue censorship. Now we come to *productivity*. s it really an effective approach to problem solving? Some people would consider this approach "working harder rather than smarter." It is the viewpoint of the old-world immigrant who believed, "if you work hard enough, you can accomplish anything." For those of us who have struggled for years, using every ounce of strength and energy to change some unwanted aspect of life with no result, there is serious doubt that such faith in this approach is justified.

Actually, productive effort is only effective if it is *aimed in exactly the right direction.* Several years ago, two highly accomplished graphic artists opened up a new graphic arts studio in San Francisco. Their intended clientele was to be the cream of the highest-priced advertising agencies in the Bay area. Both men had fine aesthetic taste and they invested heavily in creatively renovating a rustic building near Fisherman's Wharf to impress their prospective clients. They put in the finest equipment and furniture and the most modern telephone and intercom systems. Now they were ready to open for business.

There was only one problem. They had put all of their efforts (and money) into preparing their place of business. Now they needed beautifully designed and printed promotional literature and advertisements to attract customers to the masterpiece they had produced, but they couldn't afford it. They had put themselves in hock right up to their ears and couldn't squeeze out another nickel. The cheap promotional efforts they made only made them look amateurish and especially undesirable to the very high-priced clients they sought to attract. Within three months they closed their doors. Without the large volume of business they had anticipated they couldn't begin to service the large monthly debt they were committed to. They spared no cost or effort to achieve their goal, but the outcome proved that much of their effort had *gone in the wrong direction.* They proved that off-target productive effort was definitely not an effective solution. There are two questions you always have to answer:

(1) *What is the best direction in which to flow my efforts to reach my objective?* and

(2) *If I find myself going in the wrong direction, how do I change my course of action with the least possible loss of time and effort?*

Number one is mostly a question of goals, purposes, and aspirations, but number two can be a real problem:

IF YOU'VE INVESTED HEAVILY IN A DIRECTION, THAT ISN'T WORKING, HOW DO YOU LET GO AND CUT YOUR LOSSES?

Letting Go of Losers to Concentrate on Winners

The year is 1987, the month is October. The stock market falls farther than 1929. Billions are lost. The last great crash occurred in 1969, but not everyone lost. Some were smart enough to bail out before the speculative boom inevitably crashed. Gerald M. Loeb, author of *The Battle for Investment Survival,* and those who followed his advice, were some of the smart ones. Loeb advocated a formula for stock speculation based on what author Max Gunther calls, "The Ratchet Effect". A ratchet is a device which allows a notched wheel to turn forward, but stops it from slipping any farther back than the last notch on the wheel. It thus *limits losses and preserves gains.*

Loeb's investment technique worked like a ratchet. The KEY rule was that you *must* sell a stock when it has dropped 10 to 15 percent from the highest level it has reached while you owned the stock. And you must sell it then, regardless of whether you have a gain or a loss! Loeb noted, however, that few people were able to use the formula successfully. It hurt too much to follow the rule meticulously and accept the losses that quickly. Most small investors hang on, hoping the price drop is only temporary and the stock will bounce back. It's their *unrealistic optimism* that causes them to wait until their loss is drastic. In *The Luck Factor*, Max Gunther speaks of "The Pessimism Paradox." He demonstrates with story after story, the degree to which really lucky people maintain a healthy pessimism when they enter into risky investments. He says the people who most put their trust in "luck" are the least lucky. A professional gambler he quotes notes that the real mark of a "pro" is knowing how and when to get out of a hand to cut his losses.

Let's take another look at the two graphic artists who opened the studio in San Francisco, which failed in a couple of months. Is it possible that they had no indication that it might happen? At what point might they have noticed that they were getting in too deep? When should they have bailed out or changed direction? Only they can answer these questions, but it is certain that they had so much invested, they felt they couldn't afford to lose. Max Gunther calls the reader's attention to Murphy's Law: *Anything that can go wrong probably will.* He suggests that you should never go into a situation without *knowing* what you will do when things begin to go wrong.

Take a look at a problem you are having now. Are you holding on to anything which long ago lost its value, in the hope that things will turn around and you'll regain that value? Is there something you are reluctant to let go of? Even more important, is there something you could let go of which would do away with your problem altogether? It may be very painful to do so, but sooner or later you may have to let it go and accept your loss. Why not now? You won't be able to go in the right direction and build something better until you do.

Productivity and Time Management

"Great is the art of beginning, but greater is the art of ending."
                                                        Henry Wadsworth Longfellow

Production statistic: *The number of products of acceptable quality completed per unit of time.*

A study of the pressures and problems of teen-agers vs. adults found that, for teens, the greatest problem was peer pressure. For adults the greatest problem was *time pressure.* In our complex society it seems there is never enough time to do all we must, plus what we want to do. You've probably read many suggestions on, "How to increase your time," or "How to manage your time more efficiently." A problem solving text without some suggestions on controlling time wouldn't be complete. Some of these ideas may already be familiar to you, but some of them may be new and different. There's always the possibility that one of these suggestions may help you solve at least one major difficulty with time.

The problem of "not enough time" could also be stated as the problem of "not moving fast enough." If you have five bags to pack before taking a trip, and you have two days in which to pack those bags, you may complain that you "don't have enough time to pack." This probably means you have so many other things which must be done that you can't imagine packing that quickly without forgetting something vital. Visions of the trip may also intrude on your mind and add a few emotional distractions along the way. When you finally get down to the wire and have only two hours to pack before you must leave to catch your plane, you probably get into fast gear and somehow pack them in the allotted time. Deadlines have a way of speeding up one's actions, but they could also be viewed as "slowing down time." Very few people would look at it that way. Try it next time and see if that viewpoint provides you with solutions you otherwise wouldn't have thought of.

The magic KEY to solving time problems is: (1) *Prune out unnecessary tasks*, and then (2) *Complete necessary tasks or projects more quickly.* It's that simple, but simple doesn't necessari-ly mean easy. In a story on how chief executives keep track of the many factors they must monitor, *Success Magazine* reported that every successful executive lives by a detailed "TO DO" list or scheduling book. Many executives use a sophisticated *Day Timer* scheduling book. Others make lists on scraps of paper. But they all have one thing in common: they meticulously list everything which must be done, and they note which things have been completed and which have not. Some executives keep track of *how long* it takes to complete each task or project. Eventually this discipline puts real predictability into scheduling. Most executives go through their list at the end of each day, and carry forward incomplete items which must be scheduled the next day, next week, or months down the line.

Some KEYS to Preventing Inertia and Building Momentum

I have a few tricks which work well for me which I'll pass along to you. They deal directly with two major aspects of motion: *inertia* and *momentum.* "Inert" means: *Unable to move or act; resisting motion or action.* "Inertia" actually means: *The tendency of a body at rest to remain at rest, or of a body in motion to remain in motion.* But popular usage usually refers to: *Resist-ance to motion, action or change.* When we speak of positive forward motion, we usually call it "momentum".

If you're like me, first thing in the morning you're feeling very "inert." It takes quite a bit of pushing to overcome "inertia" and build some "momentum." The first trick is that completing a task or two and checking off some items on your list will tend to give you a feeling of satisfaction and build momentum. To get this feeling going, I always start with a few short tasks that I can complete right away. In that way I can start to build momentum. I'll make a few short phone calls and handle a few pieces of mail, until I feel like I'm in the swing of things. If I start out with a huge project, it may take me hours to feel I've *completed* anything. If that's all you have to work with, you can break a big project down into "bite-size" tasks and cross them off as they are completed. That should give you the same sense of satisfaction.

Another KEY to building momentum, increasing speed, and sav-ing time is to *focus on one item until you reach some point of completion.* It's easy to get started on one thing and get interrupt-ed or shifted off onto another. If you get several of these tasks or projects going at once, you can get spread so thin you'll begin to feel you'll never finish any of them. If at all possible, take on your tasks one at a time and solve your problems one at a time.

Freeing Locked-Up Attention and Building Momentum

After building some initial momentum with several short completions, the KEY to selecting your next priority (assuming there isn't some *critical* action which *must* be done first to avoid death, destruction, the I.R.S. or worse), is to choose something which is *tying up your attention* and finish that off next.

We seldom think of our concentration or attention as something finite, measurable as a quantity. But if you've ever tried to study at night when you're tired, you know what I mean when I say that you can run out of attention. Emotional confrontations or intense negotiations can *tax your attention!* Afterwards you can be too tired to concentrate. Similarly, *interruptions* can wear down the focus of your attention so that soon you will find it difficult to concentrate.

Throughout the day, the many tasks which you must face and handle can weary you and drain your attention, unless you have techniques you can use to revitalize yourself and regain your full concentration. If you quickly dispose of any issue which is claiming your attention and *distracting you* from concentrating on other things, you will accomplish much more during the rest of the day.

Tapping Into an Existing Flow

When all else fails, this last trick will often save the day. When you feel completely bogged down, stopped dead in your tracks by your own feeling of inertia, an effective strategy can be to *align with an already existing flow!* This works on little things and big things. At one point I was having a problem getting a workshop started. It seemed that no matter what I did, I just couldn't get it rolling. I put this little principle to work by getting involved with a workshop a friend already had going. That way I was able to *capitalize* on the momentum he had built up, and I was able to build enough momentum myself to start my own workshop after a short time of contributing to his.

When I was doing career counseling, I donated time to helping people who were in an alcoholism recovery program prospect for jobs. A major problem for many of them was a bad work record or no recent work record at all. Once I identified some skill a person had to offer, I would suggest that person find a charitable organization where he or she could donate that skill for a while. In this way people can get some experience, build some momentum and align with a constructive group already in motion.

If you have a problem getting some aspect of your life flowing in the right direction, ask yourself what individual or group is already flowing in that direction. Then figure out a way to align with that flow by contributing to it, until you build some momentum in the direction you wish to go.

The Sleep Factor

Since, in this chapter, we are addressing *production* and *productivity*, we are directly concerned with *time problems*. The main problem is how to complete what *must* be done, and yet do what we *want to do* in the amount of time available. There is an apparency that time is *fixed*. There are only twenty-four hours in a day and there is no known way to stretch that time (except perhaps on *Star Trek*). It would seem then, that solving a time problem is hopeless. Obviously this isn't true. There are people who complete an amazing number of tasks in business every day and still have time to jog, swim, go to the theatre, and possibly paint, write, or sculpt as well. How do they do it?

An obvious factor which determines how much we accomplish in a day is the amount of time spent sleeping. People need differing amounts of sleep. I knew a young fellow who participated in an experiment while he was in college. Participants in the experiment agreed to sleep only five hours per night for a given period of time. This friend told me that once he had conditioned himself to sleep no more than five hours, he did fine on that amount of sleep. The effect of this conditioning on his college life was quite remarkable. He was the president of his class, a competing athlete, a top scholar, and a very socially active young man. He said it seemed that he accomplished nearly twice as much as his peers.

Why Some People Sleep Less

I have made some observations, over the years, of people who get along on very little sleep as opposed to people who require a great deal of sleep. I have not quantified this information and cannot cite specific studies to support my view, but perhaps you will find that your own observations concur with mine. I have found that people who work at jobs that they do not like and who do not have other very dynamic interests which give great meaning to their lives, tend to sleep more (and indulge in escapist activities rather than creative or productive activities). I have found that people who have allowed things to pile up which are difficult to face and have retreated from facing up to these situations, will sleep longer hours, at least until they deal with the unpleasant circumstances at hand. I have also found that people who are totally dependent on others, rather than being responsible for their own lives, definitely sleep more. Finally, I have found that people who do not have a *creative* outlet in their life, or who do not make time to exercise their creative talents, sleep more.

To this I can add my own testimony: I have found that: (1) If I face up to unpleasant tasks which must be handled and get them out of the way, I sleep less and yet feel more rested; (2) If I keep elements under my own control, rather than allowing myself to become dependent on the decisions of others, I feel more awake and sleep less; and (3) If I make time to work on my creative projects every day, or at least every couple of days, I feel far more alive and vital and require less rest. Conversely, if I let that creative spark within me grow weak and fail to keep it alive, I begin to feel there is no really important purpose in living. I believe we owe it to ourselves to attend to that small voice of inspiration within. That is where the real vitality in life will be found. You will find there is no scarcity of time when approaching problems from that viewpoint, and those problems are far more likely to melt away.

Wasting, Saving and Spending Time

There is a trick to recognizing the value of time. It must be spent much in the same way we spend money. Unless you are very wealthy or very impulsive and short-sighted, you watch how you spend your money. If you have a finite amount of money to spend each week, you are careful to allocate a portion to rent, to auto, to food, to entertainment, etc. If you write checks and you are wise, you deduct each check from your balance as you go. In that way you always know approximately what your bank balance is. If you are a good money manager, you find ways to reduce your expenditures in some less desirable areas, like utilities, auto or maintenance, and thus free up additional funds to use for clothing, trips, recreation and other more desirable expenditures. Using the same basic technique, if you are capable of monitoring your use of time, you can decrease the amount of time spent on undesirable activities and increase the amount of time free for desirable activities.

Few of us ever really consider how long it takes to do most things. How long does it take you to brush your teeth? Comb your hair? Make breakfast? Drive to work? You could probably could answer at least a couple of these questions. We time some activities because we have to fit them into a schedule, but we wouldn't even think of timing most of them. None of us want to put our personal activities on a schedule, and rightly so. Nevertheless, the use of time is always a trade off. To add a new activity, you have to subtract an old one. As an experiment do the following:

1. Calculate exactly what your hourly worth really is by dividing the exact amount of time spent on your job by the exact (or average) amount of *take home* pay.

2. For at least one day, and preferably two days or even a week, keep a little notebook and write down how long it takes you to do everything: grooming, dressing, eating meals, driving, talking on the phone, watching TV-- everything!

3. Go back through your book and assign a working-time dollar-value to the time you spent on every single activity in your list of non-work activities.

4. For each activity, ask yourself, "Was that activity was actually worth that amount of time/money."

5. Look back over your activities and see how much time you devoted to exhilarating activities that made your life feel more valuable and more satisfying. Is there any way that you could spend less time on relatively unimportant things to obtain more time to spend on exhilarating activities? What problems could you solve given this additional time?

Inertia, Momentum and Emotional Stops

Take another look at these terms: "Inert" means: *Unable to move or act; resisting motion or action.* "Inertia" means *the tendency of a body at rest to remain at rest, or of a body in motion to remain in motion.* But popular usage usually refers to: *Resistance to motion, action or change.* When we speak of positive forward motion, we usually call it "momentum".

Another word which means *bodies or forces at rest* is, "static", but it also means: *Forces in equilibrium.* Picture two horses of equal strength harnessed so that each of them pulled in the *opposite* direction, using exactly the same amount of energy. You would witness an enormous amount of energy being expended with neither of the horses going anywhere. You would be seeing a perfectly balanced "tug-of-war." Now picture a person with two conflicting motivations of *equal magnitude.* With these two forces in exact equilibrium, the person would go in neither direction, but he or she would experience great stress while standing perfectly still. This picture illustrates the definition of "a psychological problem," presented in Chapter Three: "*A conflict of thoughts, emotions or other forces which result in a full or partial paralysis of constructive action."*

At one point in my life, I had a strong emotional belief that it was wrong to persuade people to do anything they didn't wish to do. At the time, I also had an opportunity to work in sales and earn money which I greatly needed for my education. Whenever I would encounter a sales prospect who expressed less than eagerness to buy my product, I would back off and not try to sell that person anything. The necessity of persuading people collided inside with my unspoken belief that, "it is always wrong to persuade." As a result my sales career ground to a halt, until I changed my belief that it was *always* wrong to attempt to persuade others to change their minds.

If you are having a problem moving in a particular direction and you feel you have encountered a "solid wall," an inner conflict, or just a "wall of inertia" that you have not been able to break through, do the following:

(1) Write down what goal you would reach if you were able to go forward, completely unobstructed.

(2) Now write down what belief could cause someone to not go in that direction.

(3) Next list the various dimensions of your personality: husband, wife, lover, employer, employee, businessperson, sportsman, student, political activist, swimmer, golfer, hobbyist, etc.

(4) Now look at each of these separate dimensions of your personality, to see if any of those identities might have the limiting belief stated in number 2 above, or may be in conflict with the identity you use to pursue the goal you feel is obstructed.

We usually act as though there is only one self—only one dimension to our personality. The fact is, however, that there are many emotional "selves." When we are with our parents, it is difficult to not see ourselves as their children, no matter how old we may be. When we're on the job, we see ourselves in our work role. When taking time to relax, most of us have a social identity which is different from our work identity. There is also the sexual self and, for many people, there is a separate moral or religious self. Two of these selves may sometimes be in conflict. If one believes that pre-marital sex is wrong, but is nevertheless strongly attracted to someone of the opposite sex to the point of having pre-marital sex, strong feelings of guilt can be attached. Two dimensions of self are in conflict. If both sides are equally strong and neither side gives in, there may be no action but one will feel the stress like the two horses pulling against one another.

In today's work of intense ambitions, the sensual, indulgent self may be in conflict with the ambitious self who wishes to earn a lot of money to buy the best. The ambitious self may hold the belief: "I deserve the best and I am willing to work as hard as I must to obtain it." The indulgent self may hold the belief: "Life is only to be enjoyed. If I feel like relaxing and doing nothing but watching TV and eating snacks, then that's what I should do." Usually one belief will dominate, but the presence of the other belief will cause stress and discomfort. A conscious choice must be made. Once you've made up your mind which belief you *really* want to prevail, a simple visualization exercise, repeated as necessary, may enable you to reduce the power of the opposing emotional attitude over your forward progress:

A Visualization Approach

a. Find a quiet, comfortable place where you won't be disturbed.

b. Imagine you have a large bag standing along side of you.

c. Recall all of the frustrations you have felt at not reaching a goal you have set for yourself.

d. Imagine that those frustrations could be made solid and placed in the bag you created along side of yourself. How big would the bag have to be to hold them? How much would it weigh with those frustrations in it?

e. Recall any efforts you have made to reach that goal—especially those that failed—and any emotional feelings of loss you had as a result of those failures.

f. Imagine that those experiences, losses, and emotional feelings could be made solid and put in the bag along with the frustrations. How tall would the bag have to be now? What would it weigh now?

g. Recall any upsets or disagreements you have had with others who may have prevented you from reaching your goal, or have just made it more difficult for you to work toward the goal.

h. Imagine that those upsets and disagreements could be made solid and placed in the same bag. How wide and how tall would the bag be now? How much would it now weigh?

i. Are there any other attitudes, beliefs, thoughts, ideas, emotional feelings or anything else which should be in the bag? If so, imagine that they could be made solid and also place them in the bag.

j. Now look at the final shape, size, and weight of the bag you have been carrying around, which has blocked the way to your goal. Create a label for that bag and place the label on the front of it.

k. Now, recognizing that this is a bag of unwanted trash, do with it exactly as you would with any bag of trash. Throw it in an imagined incinerator and watch it disintegrate into nothingness.

l. It is time now to create "a new bag." See yourself as having reached your goal and visualize the attitudes and beliefs that you now have.

m. If doing this one time does not completely eliminate the obstacle, repeat the process until it does.

Now whenever you encounter "inertia," in the form of an emotional feeling that you are stopped and can't go forward, identify what belief, attitude, feeling or other mental and emotional element would prevent you from going forward. Put them into a bag with any experiences as above. Label it and send it away to disintegrate into nothingness! If visualizing isn't effective for you, write your responses to the questions on paper. Then crumple up the paper and throw it away, discarding your unwanted feelings, attitudes and beliefs along with it. Then go on your way, newly creating the forward motion and momentum you really want!

Productivity as a KEY to Being a "SUPER SOLVER"

This chapter has mainly provided you with a collection of "tips and tricks" for faster, more efficient, productive action. Many of the problems we encounter in life could be avoided or eliminated with better planning, better organization, and better use of skills and resources. Time is foremost among those vital resources. Regardless of how good your problem solving groundwork and planning may be, you must still do the work of applying your solution. If something isn't getting done, cut back and take a smaller bite. Simple techniques like this can make the difference between solving and not solving a problem.

If you use these ideas and strategic tools to (1) Identify barriers and STOPS preventing your production flow, (2) Eliminate or overcome obstacles and inertia, and (3) Build momentum in completing what you set out to do, — you will indeed become a "Super-Solver!"

PROBLEM SOLVING POWER
CHECKLIST NUMBER 13

A. IDENTIFICATION: Confusion is often eliminated by identifying <u>exactly</u> when, what, where, why or how.

What uncertainties are stopping the flow of progress?
What confusions or perplexities are stopping the flow?
What "maybes" are stopping the flow?

Where did the flow first stop?
When were things last flowing well (if ever)?
When did it stop? What was the pivotal point?

Why did the flow stop?
Attitudes? Yours? Other's?
Emotions? Yours? Other's
Conflicts? From your point of view? From other's?
Interruptions?
 Yours? Other's?

How did it happen? (Had it happened before?)
Was something suppressed? Doubted? Withheld? Ignored?
Was something negated? Criticized? Invalidated? Rejected?
Was something distorted? Twisted? Confused? Altered? Denied?
Was something demanded? Insisted? Compelled? Protested?
What was inhibited? Delayed? Stopped?

B. ELIMINATION: Once identified, barriers and obstacles can be eliminated one at a time by recognizing and using effective strategies and tools.

To eliminate barriers and obstacles, how could you use additional:

Resources?	Expansion?
Creativity?	Production?
Knowledge?	Communication?
Motivation?	Exchange of help?

C. INTENSIFICATION: When barriers and obstacles to a forward flow have been eliminated, forward momentum can be regained and increased by intensifying determination to complete tasks quickly.

In carrying out a productive flow to reach your ideal objective, what have you:

Delegated? Re-scheduled?
Dismissed or discarded completely?
Accelerated?
Completed?

Space expansion power requires a willingness to explore.

Often we must take risks to reach out and
discover new ways to solve problems.

14. EXPANSION POWER

"A management needs a rational growth policy. . . What is the minimum of growth without which the company would actually lose strength, vigor, and ability to perform, if not to survive? . . . The second growth objective needed is an optimum objective. What is the combination of activities, products and businesses that promises to produce the best balance between risk and return on resources?"

— Peter Drucker
Management: Tasks, Responsibilities, Practices

Expand: *1. To open up or out; spread out; unfold. 2. To increase the dimensions of. 3. To increase the scope of; extend; develop.*

Observation: *Anything that isn't growing is dying. Nothing stays the same.*

Corollary: *Any program, project or activity that isn't improving will begin to deteriorate.*

Special problem definition: *Any factor contributing to a decline or deterioration could be considered to be "a problem." A problem may be defined by the degree to which it prevents progress toward an objective, or the degree to which it contributes power to movement in the opposite direction, away from the objective.*

Corollary: *Any existing situation which is* <u>less than ideal</u> *has growth and improvement potential.* <u>Any obstacle</u> *to continued growth or improvement could therefore be considered to be* <u>a problem</u>.

Hypothesis: *Any problem can be solved with sufficient growth and expansion.*

You May Have a Problem You Didn't Know You Had

When I give a seminar on problem solving power, I ask attendees to make a list of problems they would like to solve *before* they come to the seminar. I do this because I've found that, amazingly, many people find it difficult to think of a problem on the spur of the moment. Over a cup of coffee with a friend, these same people easily come up with many problems to discuss. When asked to take a systematic approach to problem solving, however, they quickly pass over gigantic portions of their lives which they find less than satisfactory. It seems that:

> WHEN A PROBLEM IS TOO LARGE FOR AN INDIVIDUAL
> TO EVEN CONCEIVE OF A SOLUTION, IT MAY NOT
> BE PERCEIVED AS "A PROBLEM."

A common example is the single person who has nearly abandoned the hope of ever finding a mate. When you ask this person for problems, the subject will never come up. It has been dismissed as "impossible." A similar situation is the individual who has worked in a dead-end job for so long, the possibility of leaving it and moving into a truly desirable job no longer crosses his or her mind. In the earlier chapter entitled, "Why Problems Don't Get Solved," I presented a spectrum of "The Stages of Growth and Decline:"

↑ GROWTH:	↓ DECLINE:
8. MAXIMIZE	CULMINATE
7. CAPITALIZE	DISSIPATE
6. UTILIZE	STAGNATE
5. ORGANIZE	DISINTEGRATE
4. ENERGIZE	SEPARATE
3. FAMILIARIZE	TERMINATE
2. REVIEW/REVISE	SPECTATE
1. RECOGNIZE	FABRICATE

By the time a problem has dropped to "stagnate" or lower, on the decline side, it may be difficult to reverse the situation. When a problem gets this big, it's like a big, old, overweight pet elephant. It just lies there and takes up space, and you have to keep walking around it. You may be one of those individuals, stuck at one of these points of decline. Like the worker in the dead-end job, you may be stuck at "stagnate." Or like the bachelor or spinster who can't find a mate, this circumstance may keep you "separated" from desired activities. After "terminating" the search for a lover, a better job, a more desirable place to live, or more interesting friends, you may just resign yourself to "spectating" rather than living.

Many people cannot deal with problems of this magnitude at all. They begin to "fabricate" a world of illusion and unreality. In years gone by, you would find them wandering around the grounds of mental institutions with a dazed look in their eyes. Today, you may find them pushing a shopping cart down the street,

- 186 -

filled with their belongings. The problem becomes too painful to even *spectate,* and so they withdraw from life into a totally *fabricated* reality. It is unlikely that your problems are this serious, but, if your focus is not on growth and expansion, they may eventually become more serious than you would ever imagine.

The Pain of Growth: Why People Choose Not to Change

Intellectually you probably agree with the words of Cardinal Newman I quoted earlier in the book: *"Growth is the only evidence of life."* You look around you and see that we can differentiate plants and animals from rocks and soil, because the living things *grow!* If a plant or a child does not grow, we assume it is sick. Generally speaking we think of growth as "good," and decline or decay as "bad." What would you say if I told you that you may be *trying not to grow* in some area of your life?

An aspect of growth that we tend to ignore is the fact that *growth is often painful.* Remember the years of your childhood just before you became a teenager. These years of puberty are sometimes called the "ugly duckling" years. They are the painful years of growth which precede the transformation from the ugly duckling into the beautiful swan. Bodies do not grow smoothly. They grow in spurts and jumps. Parts of the body are stretched and distorted. During periods of rapid growth, children can feel "growing pains."

Businesses, careers, and personal life-styles can encounter the "pain of growth" also. Growth is especially painful after a level plateau of relative success or even mediocrity has been established for a long time. As this is being written in 1988, the Soviet Union is going through a major attempt to restructure economic patterns in their society. After decades of party-dominated production quotas, patterns of stagnation have become entrenched. The new attempt to turn to personal initiative and profit-oriented incentives is causing great stress. When the main reason growth has been prevented or limited has been the influence of top management (as in the case of the Communist Party in Russia), often the only way expansive change can be achieved is to *alter or remove top management.* Mikhail Gorbachev, the new Soviet leader, has begun the process of reducing the influence of the Communist Party on the Soviet economy, thereby giving more power to the working people to make changes which will lead to economic growth. Will he succeed? Will they survive the "pain of growth"? Only time will tell.

A powerful example in the U.S. business world was Thomas Watson Sr., the founder of IBM. For years Watson ran his company internally on a basis of managerial austerity. He had no staffs, no research and development division, and no vice presidents. There was only the top man: Thomas Watson. For years Watson prepared IBM to be a big company. His viewpoint was constantly, "If you want to be a big company tomorrow, you have to start acting like one today." When the time for the major transition to a large corporation came, however, Watson did not want to step aside and let younger men take over. Peter Drucker states the problem succinctly:

> For a company to be able to grow, top management must be willing and able to change itself, its role, its relationship and its behavior. This is easily said—and very hard to accomplish.
>
> The very people—and usually the very man—of whom such change is demanded are also, as a rule, the people to whom the success of the company so far can be attributed. Now, when success is within their grasp, they are asked to abandon the behavior that has produced it. They are asked—or so it seems to them—to abdicate their leadership position. They are asked, above all, to hand over their "child" to others.
>
> . . . Growth always requires that the management of one man—or of a small handful of men—be replaced by a genuine top-management team.

To bring positive change into a stagnant or disintegrating situation, you will probably have to change the thinking *at the top!* Even within yourself it may not be enough to tinker with changing a small habit pattern or two. You may have to revise your entire philosophy or approach to life. I have known some incredibly overweight people who slimmed down, and thus greatly improved their social lives. These major changes in weight were not accomplished by giving up a snack or two or skipping a meal a day. All of these people had to *totally revise their eating habits.* Before the change could occur in their daily eating habits, these people had to make a mental change "at the top." They had to accept the reality of a new kind of personal management and to make a commitment to maintaining that management until they reached their objective. By that time the new management style (in their case just eating-management) had become a new habitual pattern, and so they were able to sustain it.

It is an inescapable fact: *growth always requires change*, and whenever the possibility of change brings with it the risk of losing power, comfort, or security, many people will resist that change. They may prefer stagnation, limitation, and even relative dissatisfaction, to the untested, uncertain possibility of a better future.

It is also a fact that change will eventually come, no matter how hard we resist it. Far better that we take control of the change process now and guide it while we can, rather than finding one day that undesirable change has crept up on us while we were trying to cling to an outmoded, comfortable pattern.

RECOGNIZING THE DEGREE OF GROWTH OR DECLINE
(and thus the degree of urgency of the problem)

Observation: Growth occurs on a gradual, if erratic, upward curve, passing through clearly definable stages. *Decline* usually occurs on a gradual downward curve, but there is always a far greater potential for *rapid* or even *instant* decline and destruction, than for rapid or instant growth. Buildings which took months or years to build can be burned or bombed to the ground in hours.

Growth can be as much of a problem as decline. An already wealthy man won a large sum of money in a sweepstakes. "Damn!" he said, "That's really going to complicate my tax situation!" Most of us would like very much to have that problem. We would much rather take on the task of working out what to do with extra income than trying to figure out how to get by with too little income. In general we look forward to solving problems of growth, and we dread facing up to solving problems of decline. If we can solve a problem of growth, we will get ahead. If we solve a problem of decline, we won't fall back any farther, but we may also feel no farther ahead.

At each stage of growth or decline, there is a problem solving strategy which stands the best chance of eliminating any stops on the upward curve toward an objective, or preventing further decline away from the objective. It would be presumptuous of me to dogmatically state that the strategies in this book are absolutely the best solutions available. I wouldn't suggest that the checklist which follows this chapter contains the *only* effective approach to problem solving, but it summarizes most of the strategies which have worked well for me, and I have observed them work well for others. I believe they will work well for you if you apply them. That's the best I can offer.

I have emphasized all along that the first step in any endeavor is to *recognize* who you are, where you are, why you're there, where you're going, and when and how. The stages of growth and decline are simply a model to help you identify how close or how far you are from reaching an objective. Another way of looking at this model is to break it down into *zones* of operation:

ZONE:	GROWTH:	DECLINE:	ZONE:
Power Zone	Maximize Capitalize	Culminate Dissipate	*Caution* Zone
Normal Zone	Utilize Organize	Stagnate Disintegrate	*Attention* Zone
Critical Zone	Energize Familiarize	Separate Terminate	*Crisis* Zone
Preliminary Zone	Review/Revise Recognize	Spectate Fabricate	*Sub-survival* Zone

Each zone of operation calls for a different problem-solving strategy. The checklist at the end of this chapter may be the most vital and valuable of all for you on a day-to-day basis. Every moment of your life you are pursuing some objective, even if it is only "to have fun," or "to relax." When you are pursuing that objective, you are always at some point in the spectrum of growth or decline.

Let's take a sample problem like, "How to have a good time this evening." You may have already *recognized* that you want to have a good time. You quickly *review* times you have enjoyed yourself, and decide what you want to do for the evening. You *familiarize* yourself with the options: available restaurants, entertainment, and perhaps choices of escort. You then *energize* your plan by calling and making reservations, confirming times or making a date. During your calls you *organize* where you will go, approximately when, and in what sequence. Then you *utilize* your plan and go out to have a good time. You will *capitalize* on any additional opportunities which come along, like meeting some other friends or discovering some new entertainment along the way. If your plan works out well, you will have *maximized* your potential for fun on your evening out.

Whatever your project may be, if you run into a snag somewhere along the way, it is always helpful to know what stage of development got "hung up." Even in choosing social or recreational activities, you will predictably have more enjoyment if you *recognize* what you *really enjoy doing* that you can do rather than *fabricating* or fantasizing about unrealistic and unattainable activities. You may have more fun if you *review* what you have enjoyed and you make your own choices, rather than being a passive *spectator* while others make recreational choices for you. It may take a bit of work to *familiarize* yourself with the options, rather than giving up and *terminating* the idea of choosing to have a good time. But *energizing* even as simple a project as an evening out is better than *separating* yourself out from satisfying social contact with others.

This tool applies in every aspect of life. When you see your job, your business, or your marriage begin to *disintegrate*, if you know that there is a specific strategy to *organize* new growth and improvement, it will give you hope to continue forward. If you have begun to *stagnate* in your job, business, marriage, or other relationship, you will find strength in knowing that there is a strategy to *utilize* hidden resources, creativity, knowledge and enthusiasm to get moving again. If you have *dissipated* (wasted) an opportunity to advance in your career, business, economic, or social endeavors, it is helpful to know there is a strategy you can call on to *capitalize* on the next opportunity which arises. Unlimited future vistas are opened up by the knowledge that you do not have to "peak out," or *culminate,* but rather that you have a strategy to *maximize* your potential and sustain growth throughout your life.

The Problem-Solving Power of Growth and Expansion

Long-term problems are seldom solved by "playing it safe." You must risk reaching out into new spaces, places, groups, activities and games to find new viewpoints and new solutions. I hope you find the following checklist a useful tool to help you do reach out smoothly, comfortably and effectively.

PROBLEM SOLVING POWER

CHECKLIST NUMBER FOURTEEN

PRELIMINARY STEP: Identify the zone which encompasses your stage of progress or decline. Apply the strategies for that zone.

ORIENTATION ZONE

Problem Condition:
Direction of endeavor unknown or uncertain.

Strategy — **Recognize, Don't Fabricate:**
(Key = Honest self-appraisal)

In terms of your proposed endeavor, (1) *Where* are you right now? (2) *Where* would you like to be. (3) *Who* are you right now? (4) *Who* would you like to be? (5) *How* motivated are you to pursue this endeavor? (6) *What* can you learn from attempting to reach this objective, regardless of whether you reach it or not? (7) *What* are your chances of carrying the endeavor through to a completion? (8) *What* do you stand to lose if it doesn't work? If it does work? (9) *What* do you stand to win if it does work? If it doesn't work? (10) If you carry out the project, *who* will be helped? Will anyone be harmed?

Strategy — **Review/Revise, Don't Spectate:**
(Key = Unflinching review and inspection)

(1) Review the history which preceded this problem: What are the circumstances which led up to it? When were things last going well? When did they stop going well? Has this problem occurred in the past? What led up to it then? Was it solved then? How? Who was responsible for solving it? Is that person still around to answer questions? Gather as many facts as you can from other times and places.

(2) Examine all of the *present* circumstances surrounding the problem situation: Who are the people involved in the problem? Who has the power to make decisions? Who do people follow? What questions can you get answers to? Find out all of the facts you can. Do surveys. Do interviews. Take people to lunch. Compare your situation to other individuals, groups, departments, companies, etc. If you can't get answers to direct questions, find out the answers indirectly. Contact, call or write friends, business associates, competitors — *anybody!*

(3) Look at the *future* consequences of every course of action you might try while attempting to resolve the problem: What solutions have you already tried? What happened? Is it likely to happen again? What would happen if your solution worked perfectly? Would anyone be unhappy with the outcome? Would anyone refuse to try the solution you suggest? Is there any way you could prepare people for changes you might propose in trying to solve the problem? Is the solution you are considering just a temporary fix which might result in the problem coming back in the future?

CRITICAL ZONE

Problem Condition: You are bordering on either launching or abandoning an entire project. Probability of success highly uncertain; probability of failure is unpleasantly high. There are many unknowns. The existence and identity of possible support personnel is unknown and/or uncertain.

Strategy — **Familiarize, Don't Terminate:**

(Key = Thoroughness!)

(1) Communicate —Find out what individuals (and groups) you should talk to if you are going to reach your objective.

(2) Knowledge — Determine what you most need to know to resolve your problem and reach your objective.

(3) Resources — Sort out exactly what tools, equipment, finances, personnel, energy sources, spaces and time you will need to get the job done.

(4) Help/Contribute: — As part of your search for resources, find out what person or persons would be most willing and able to help you reach your objective. Also find out what you could offer in exchange for that help.

(5) Create — Design a clever plan to get in touch with the people you must contact, to gather the information you need and to obtain the resources and help you will need. List the actions needed to carry out your plan in order of importance (most important first, least important last).

(6) Produce — Carry out your familiarization plan, step - by - step. *Key = In-depth* application of vital steps!

(7) Morale — To keep your spirits and motivation up, work as quickly as possible through the steps of the plan, completing each step thoroughly as you go (completions build enthusiasm). Reschedule incomplete steps for a very *specific* future time.

(8) Expansion — Reach out in a widening circle to every pertinent source of information, resources, help and inspiration until you feel confident you have assembled what you need to reach your objective and to overcome any inclination to give up or quit.

Strategy — Energize, Don't Separate:
(Key = Speed, persistence and cooperation)

(1) Knowledge — Recognize the seriousness of this critical zone; perceive and grasp the facts quickly! Do a rapid assessment of your skills, knowledge, talents and abilities to establish any lack of ability to handle the situation. Draw on other's knowledge and experience to put power behind critical handling measures.

(2) Communicate — Ask for any help available; communicate the urgency of the situation; call for unified action.

(3) Create — Quickly seek innovative ideas, solutions and available courses of action. Generate instant inspiration and creativity in all concerned.

(4) Produce — Carry out emergency measures quickly to avoid a crisis situation or a recurrence of a crisis situation.

(5) Resources — Commit *all* resources to getting any crisis under control. Do not hold back! Ask for help from every available quarter. Cancel all wasteful or unnecessary use of resources! (Allow no half-hearted measures!).

(6) Expansion — Reach out to every possible source of power. Who has successfully handled a critical situation like this before? Encompass a larger space, larger possibilities, greater dimensions. Address a wider frame of reference.

(7) Morale — Resolve inner and outer conflicts. Confront your anxieties and other negative emotions; release them in any healthful way that you can. Recognize the possibilities of loss or failure, but don't dwell on them. Focus *all* attention on positive, productive possibilities and concentrate your energy with full intensity on one target at a time.

(8) Help/Contribute — Challenge the tendency to fixate on a "self-solution." Include everyone possible! Direct a flow of power, help and guidance to anyone who can contribute to a solution.

NORMAL CAUTION ZONE

Problem Condition: Occasional or regular decline in productive output, income, growth or expansion.

Strategy — **Organize, Don't Disintegrate:**

(Key = Orderly correction)

(1) Knowledge — Remove confusion from your environment as much as possible. Organize information. Open up new areas of knowledge and upgrade or stabilize existing skills.

(2) Communicate — Update files, mail lists, contacts. Handle any outstanding upsets or disagreements. Output large quantities of communication and/or promotion.

(3) Create — Create more efficient procedures. Develop a better image on correspondence, promotion, presentations and appearance.

(4) Produce — Increase all income or advantage producing activities. Cut out unproductive activities. Eliminate inefficiency as much as you can. Step up the pace of productivity. Complete incomplete actions and projects as soon as possible.

(5) Resources — Economize on expenditures of resources and consolidate your debts. Collect all monies owed you. Sell off or discard space-consuming unneeded tools, equipment, furniture and other objects. Budget resources with greater emphasis on income and accumulation of resources.

(6) Expansion — Expand time and energy devoted to resource-producing activities. Organize outreach activities to develop a larger support group of helpers, suppliers, professional advisors and friends.

(7) Morale — Eliminate unproductive, energy-draining connections and obligations. Organize procedures to discipline, strengthen, and reward activities which will increase orderly production and reduce any tendency toward confusion or disintegration.

(8) Help/Contribute: — Broaden the definition of your activity to include a contribution to a wider sphere of humanity.

Strategy — **Utilize, Don't Stagnate:**

(Key = Focus on positive change opportunities)

(1) Avoid becoming indifferent and stagnant in your efforts to resolve problems which block your higher aspirations.

Continually look for new avenues to explore and possible new beginnings where you can make better use of your creativity, productivity, resources, marketing reach, knowledge, communication, enthusiasm and altruistic spirit.

(2) Do a routine quality check to see if errors, false information, or destructive behavior and communication have damaged your forward progress. Prune out and eliminate poisonous people, negative communications and counter-productive attitudes as soon as you discover them.

(3) Avoid becoming stuck in unfinished tasks and projects by following through and either completing, delegating, rescheduling or abandoning each of them as soon as you see a pattern of stagnation beginning. Fully *utilize* all available talents, skills, people and resources to reach targetted objectives.

POTENTIAL POWER ZONE

Problem Situation: In the past sudden good fortune and unexpected opportunities have slipped through your fingers. This time you want to be certain to *capitalize* on a stroke of luck and to *maximize* the momentary advantage of your position.

Strategy — **Capitalize, Don't Dissipate:**
 (Key = Humility; Realize fragility of advantage)

(1) Resources — Avoid the tendency to waste sudden strokes of good fortune. Immediately economize on the use of new resources. Eliminate past liabilities and consolidate new growth by paying off outstanding obligations.

(2) Communicate — Eliminate past personal liabilities by correcting any outstanding upsets. Reinforce and consolidate connections with powerful communication contacts. Then expand the scope of your communications.

(3) Knowledge — Research information on (a) investment of your new resources, and (b) on opportunities to increase skills to further develop your productive potential.

(4) Create — Design a plan to accelerate growth to a new, higher plateau of accomplishment. Use increased momentum to inspire even more creative growth innovations.

(5) Morale — Capitalize on your momentary good fortune and enthusiasm to motivate yourself and others to greater accomplishments. Do not *dissipate* your forward momentum! Focus on the fact that rapid forward motion builds enthusiasm. Becoming complacent slows and sometimes stops that momentum and leads to lethargy and decline. Maintain high momentum and morale!

(6) Produce — Implement your plan to accelerate growth and complete the steps in your plan quickly to discourage interruptions and distractions while building even greater forward momentum!

(7) Help/Contribute: — Broaden the definition of your increased activity to include a greater contribution to a wider sphere of humanity.

(8) Expansion — Avoid becoming self-satisfied with your momentary advantage. Continue to reach out widely for new contacts and opportunities. Use your increased momentum and good fortune to greatly widen your sphere (and/or your group's sphere) of influence and accomplishment.

Strategy — **Maximize, Don't Culminate:**

(Key = Sharing power to increase power)

(1) Avoid peaking out and coming to the end of your growth phase just because you have finished resolving one problem or reached one major objective. Create new efforts to resolve larger problems which may be blocking even higher aspirations, by continually looking for possible new beginnings and new avenues to explore.

(2) Continue to grow by building on the solid base you have established, even if you shift into a completely new activity. Offer the techniques which have worked for you on a individual, family or company level to others to help resolve the larger problems of society around you and in the world.

(3) Establish long-term continuance of the success you have created by communicating what you have learned through writing books, making tapes, videos and films, or delivering seminars, workshops, apprenticeships and courses.

Compile your most effective problem-solving strategies when you don't need them, and you'll have them when you do.

15. SUMMING UP

Man is not the sum of what he has but the totality of what he does not yet have, of what he might have been.

—*Jean Paul sartre*

So here we are at the end of the problem solving process or, should I say, at the end of the training and the beginning of the real process? I have presented you with a smorgasbord of problem solving methods. If you have followed along through the text this far, you have a right to ask what I personally consider the *most* important technique (and even if you don't ask, I'd like to tell you). Personally, I believe that *creativity* is the heart of problem solving, in two ways:

1. Generally problems of the sort we're looking at in the context of this book (career, business and personal goal problems), don't just happen; they are created. I believe your first vital task is to find out *who or what is responsible for creating the problem!* It may be someone else. It may be you. If it seems someone else is mainly responsible for creating it, then your next vital task is to recognize *what part of the problem you are responsible for creating,* even if it's only a small part. You have limited power over the actions of others but, with determination and persistence, you can change what *you are doing.* Then, with cleverly applied tact and skill, you may be able to also change what others are doing. When you have properly identified the source of your problem, then you can create a solution that will *strike at the very heart of the problem* and resolve that problem in the shortest possible time.

2. After gathering the input of information, special knowledge and skills, plus the resources of time, space, money, motivation, and human help, the KEY to solving the problem is *a creatively designed sequence of actions which result in the desired solution.* This one sentence sums it up, but it is a convergence of all of the techniques described in this book. They are all the ingredients that you, the master-chef solver, need to cook up together in your final creative masterpiece: the effective solution.

Solutions vary in quality, like cars, clothes, and cuisine. A minimally effective solution is one that gets you out of a jam, at least temporarily. A decent solution gets you out of a jam permanently, usually by allowing you to reorganize the problem dimension of your life so the problem doesn't occur again. An ideal solution is one that not only solves your problem, but also enables people with similar problems, wherever they may be, to arrive at a solution, or perhaps to avoid the problem altogether.

A Super-Solver Who Changed the Entire World

Few would deny that the computer has changed the world. In the last fifteen years, the *personal computer* has taken the power to make major changes out of the exclusive hands of governments, the military, and big business, and put it in the hands of any individual with a thousand dollars and an ability to read and follow a few instructions.

One individual has been a major creative driving force behind this capability, and he has become a billionaire in the process. He did not accomplish this miracle single-handedly, but he did pull together some of the best creative minds and resources in the world. He then focused them on solving pivotal problems which will change our lives well into the next century. If you're not familiar with the computer industry, you may never have heard of Bill Gates. But, it has been said, that even current IBM chairman John Akers looks to Microsoft, the company Bill Gates created, as a model.

In 1980, IBM gave Microsoft the opportunity to create the operating system for IBM's Personal Computer, which has since become the standard for the entire personal computer industry. That operating system, commonly referred to as "MS-DOS," is in use in the vast majority of personal computers *throughout the world.* By 1983, Bill Gates was able to obtain the best in creative management help to make Microsoft grow. By then he could afford to hire Jon A. Shirley away from the powerful Tandy Corporation (Radio Shack, etc.), to become president of Microsoft. This increased corporate revenues by $50 million dollars. From that point on, the climb was straight up. In 1984, Microsoft introduced a KEY product for the Apple MacIntosh: the *Excel* spreadsheet. Revenues leaped by $97 milllion. In 1985, Gates introduced another breakthrough called *Windows*—a program for the IBM which gave it a new visual dimension to rival the MacIntosh. Revenues shot up $198 million. In 1987, IBM adopted the *Windows* technology as part of the operating system for their new line of personal computers, yielding $346 million for Microsoft.

If problem solving success was measured only in dollars, with $590 million in revenues after just thirteen years in business, Bill Gates would be an uncontested super-solver, but he has been much more than that. He has drawn together some of the most innovative minds available, and retained those talents with a creative management approach which equals his company's technological innovations. Compare some of his approaches to the elements of the "Octagon"

I've asked you to consider throughout this book:

Using the Octagon to Manage Other Solvers

Communication: Listening is the heart of communication and Bill Gates has made certain that his company excels at that skill. Both marketing and technical people listen to customers and *ask for problems*. In the computer industry, every product is updated with a new version on a regular basis. If a company is listening well, the new version solves the problems of the old version without introducing new problems. A top requirement for any effective solution is that the solution should not create a new problem. Communication is the KEY tool to keep that from happening.

Productivity Speed: In an industry where ideas are a product, the *speed of exchange* of those ideas determines how quickly they can be translated into a saleable product. At Microsoft a computerized communication system, called *electronic mail*, instantly speeds ideas, memos, and every kind of communication from a sender to his or her selected recipients. For most people, procrastination keeps problems persisting, when quick action and communication could have resolved them at a very early stage. Keeping *speed* of production as a high priority, without sacrificing quality, requires the kind of balancing that Bill Gates achieves at Microsoft. Mastering the ability to maintain that kind of balance will soon move you up to "Super-Solver" class as well.

Knowledge Resources: At Microsoft, *selectivity* is the KEY. We have seen that there are people who are *super-solvers* and people who are *super problems*. False assumptions and inadequate information *create* problems. Microsoft sends developers to campuses to recruit only the sharpest new minds. To resolve a critical problem, you have seek out the very best information that you can. Errors in selecting information sources are the worst of all possible errors. Gates says at Microsoft the amount of time spent on recruiting is incredible, but it has obviously paid off. The implication is obvious: If you put your best efforts into the earliest stages of the process, the final steps will far easier and will make up for the time invested early on.

Personal (Personnel) Morale: Many of the top personnel at Microsoft have become wealthy in their own right. When money is no longer a primary motivation, there must be other rewards which are even more meaningful, to retain good talent. Many companies insist on promoting creative people by moving them into management. Gates says he learned his best lessons by working at other software companies and seeing what they did wrong. He says they didn't listen

- 201 -

to people and didn't choose people carefully. He wanted to start a business where people *enjoyed working* and were able to be creative. He allows creative people to have fun doing what they do best. If they excel, they can achieve a top creative status called "architect."

Although production deadlines have to be met on a regular basis, in between projects creative "retreats" are organized where ideas can be freely exchanged and creative "batteries" can be recharged. Problems seem to develop in an *atmosphere of extremes*. Extreme discipline and extreme freedom both lead to problems in children. The results obtained at Microsoft and similar companies suggest that motivating others to help solve problems is a balancing act. The freedom to create is carefully balanced with a disciplined structure which gets things done and rewards accomplishment.

Creative Expansion: At Microsoft, the weekend escapes, called "Innovation Retreats," form the basis for new product exploration. Gates says the weekend includes a mix of formal presentations and informal discussions. These events are scheduled many months in advance. Major decisions which determine the future direction of a product line can come out of a weekend retreat. Gates has demonstrated perfectly the importance of establishing a special space in which to create. Without a planned "creative space," people try to solve problems "on the fly." Although many of the tactics presented in this book will work well to provide a "quick fix," a long-term strategy requires real creative thought. Gates takes his people out to an old big house in the islands of Puget Sound. You can use any space that works for you, but the best creative thought seems to occur away from the day-to-day pressures which claim so much of one's attention.

The Firm Grip

Tennis was my favorite game for many years. I played only casually for fun and so invested very little time in taking lessons. My biggest problem was weak wrists and a weak grip. My main interests in life were writing and music, neither of which did much to give me a strong grasp on a tennis racket. Early on, when I would go to hit the ball, the racket would twist in my hand and the ball would fly off, completely out of control. Somehow it took quite a while for me to realize that my biggest problem was the lack of a *firm grip*.

I've noticed that people often approach games the way they approach life. Impulsive game players tend to live their lives impulsively as well. Cautious, conservative players are generally conservative in most dimensions of their lives. At that time in my life, I lacked a "firm grip" in just about every sense of the word. I don't recall whether I first noticed the importance of developing a firm grip in life or in tennis, but I do know that it made a major difference in both. It also began to change how I approached solving problems.

A problem, by definition, is a difficult situation, filled with confusions and uncertainties. The worst problems come at you fast and require an immediate response. Some of my early tennis opponents had a powerful serve. Even when I was able to connect with their bullet-ball serves, I had to maintain a mighty grip on my racket to even get the ball back over the net. The harder and faster the problem coming your way, the stronger your grip must be to deal with it. Many people handle difficult problems like I handled a fast ball during my early tennis returns. Like the ball, they kind of bounce off from the problem in some random direction and wind up in the bushes.

Creative design and management are definitely my choice for first place in the problem solving arsenal, but next is follow-through, another important tennis skill. A good friend, who has been a management consultant for many years, complained to me that the worst part of his job was the fact that many of the consultation reports he developed wound up in a drawer or on a shelf and were never used. Corporations (and governments) have spent millions on studies and reports, and then put them on the shelf and continued on in the same inefficient, unproductive fashion. In tennis, part of the secret of maintaining a firm grip and a powerful swing is to *follow though* with that swing.

If you have put together a list of problem solving tactics and strategies that you feel will work for you, don't put them in a drawer or on the shelf. Put them to use right now. Schedule a definite time when you will take that next action. When that time comes, do what you planned. If you find, when you get to that time, that you have underestimated what you need, reschedule your next step for a new definite time. Don't allow your solving measures to become vague. Maintain a firm grip and a good follow through. Soon you'll find you've become a super-solver, and every solution you serve drives your problems completely out of the court!

PROBLEM SOLVING POWER
YOUR OWN CHECKLIST

APPENDIX 1 — BIBLIOGRAPHY

Ackoff, Russell Lincoln-"The Art of Problem-Solving"
    1978-Wiley & Sons - New York
Adams, James L.-"The Care and Feeding of Ideas"
    1986-Addison Wesley - Morrow Hill, NY
Addeo, Edmond G.-"EgoSpeak: Why no one listens to you"
    1973-Chilton Book Co - Radnor, PA
Albrecht, Karl-"Brain Power"
    1980-Prentice-Hall - Englewood Cliffs, NJ
Berlo, David K. — "The Process of Communication" — 1960,
    Holt, Rinehart & Winston — San Francisco, CA.
Berne M.D., Eric-"Games People Play." 1964-Random House - New York, NY
Blotnick, Srully Ph.D.-"Getting Rich Your Own Way"
    1980- Doubleday & Co., Inc.; Garden City, New York
Barnett, Harold J. & Chandler Morse-"Scarcity and Growth: The Ecomonics of Natural
    Natural Resource Availability. 1963-John Hopkins Press - Baltimore, MD
Bransford, John-"The Ideal Problem-Solver: A guide for improving thinking,
    learning and creativity." 1984-W.H. Freeman - New York, NY
Brothers, Dr. Joyce-"How to Get Whatever You Want Out of Life"
    1978 - Random House/Ballantine Books; New York, NY
Bryn-Jones, David-"The Dilemma of the Idealist"
    1954-MacMillan, New York
Chaplin, J.P.-"Dictionary of Psychology." (3rd Rev.) 1985- Dell - New York, NY
Clark, Malcolm-"Perplexity and Knowledge: An inquiry into the
    structuring of questioning" 1972-Nijholf, The Hague
Conklin, Robert-"How to Get People to Do Things"
    1979-Contemporary Books - Chicago, IL
Crosby, Philip B.-"Quality Without Tears"
    1984-McGraw-Hill - New York, NY
Crovitz, Dr. Herbert F.-"The Creativity Question"
Davis, Gary A.-"The Psychology of Problem Solving"
    1973-Basic Books - New York, NY
De Bono, Edward-"The Five-Day Course in Thinking"
    1967-Basic Books - New York, NY
De Bono, Edward-"New Think: The Use of Lateral Thinking"
    1968-Basic Books - New York, NY
Dobson, Terry & Victor Miller-"Giving In To Get Your Way" - 1978,
    Delacorte Press; 1 Dag Hammerskjold Plaza, New York, NY
Drucker, Peter F.-"Management: Tasks, Responsibilities, Practices"
    1974-Harper & Rowe - New York - San Francisco - London
Ehrenberg, Miriam & Otto-"Optimum Brain Power"
    1985-Dodd, Mead & Co. - 79 Madison Ave., New York, NY 10016
Eisenberg, Abne M.-"Living Communication"
    1975-Prentice-Hall - Englewood Cliffs, NJ
Flew, Dr. Anthony-"Thinking Straight." (American Edition 1977)
    Prometheus Books - 923 Kensington Ave., Buffalo, NY 14215
Gallwey, W. Timothy-"The Inner Game of Tennis"
    1974-Random House - New York, NY
Gendlin, Eugene T.-"Focusing." (Revised) 1981-Bantam Books - New York, NY
Gunther, Max-"The Luck Factor"
    1977- MacMillan Publishing Co., Inc.; 866 3rd Ave., N.Y., NY
Hanneman, Gerhard J. & Wiliam J. McEwen — "Communication and Behavior"
    1975, Addison-Wesley Pub. Co.; Menlo Park, CA.
Harris M.D., Thomas A.-"I'm O.K.—You're O.K." 1967-Harper & Row - New York, NY
Harrison, Allen F., and Robert M. Bramson, PhD-Syles of Thinking"
    1982-Anchor Press/Doubleday - Garden City, NY
Hayes, John R.-"The Complete Problem-Solver"
    1981-Franklin Institute Press - Philadelphia, PA
Heun, Linda R. & Richard E.-"Developing Skills for Human Interaction"
    1975-C.E. Merrill Publishing Co. - Columbus, OH
Jackson, Keith F.-"The Art of Solving Problems"
    1975-St. Martin's Press - New York, NY
Jorgensen, James D.-"Solving Problems in Meetings"
    1981-Nelson-Hall, Chicago Ill
Kepner, Charles Higgins-"The Rational Manager: A Systematic Approach to Problem
    Solving & Decision Making." 1965:McGraw-Hill - New York, NY

Kleinmuntz, Benjamin, Ed.-"Problem Solving Research: Method & Theory"
    1965 Symposium: Carnegie Institute of Technology. 1966-Wiley & Sons, NY, NY
Koberg, Don-"The Universal Traveler: A Soft Systems Guide to Creativity"
    1974-W.Kaufmann, Publishers - Los Altos, CA
Kohler, Heinz-"Scarcity Challenged"
    1963-Holt, Rinehart & Winston - New York
Levinstein, Aaron-"Use Your Head: The New Science of Personal
    Problem Solving." 1965-Wiley & Sons - New York, NY
Lewis, David & James Greene-"Thinking Better"
    1982-Rawson, Wade Publishers, Inc. - New York, NY
Mahoney, Michael J.-"Self-Change Strategies for Solving"
    1979-Norton - New York, NY
Mayer, Richard E.-"Thinking, Problem Solving, Cognition"
    1983-W.H. Freeman - New York, NY
Newell, Allen-"Human Problem-Solving"
    1972-Prentice-Hall - Englewood Cliffs, NJ
Moore, Linda Perigo-"You're Smarter Than You Think"
    1985-Holt, Rinehart & Winston, Publishers-An Owl Book
Newman, James W.-"Release Your Brakes." 1977-Warner Books - New York, NY
Nichols, Ralph G. Ph.D. & Leonard A. Stevens-"Are You Listening?"
    1957 - McGraw-Hill Book Company; New York-Toronto-London
Ohmae, Kenichi-"The Mind of the Strategist"
    1982-McGraw-Hill Book Co., New York, NY
Osborn, Alex F.-"Way Beyond the I.Q."
Ozer, Mark N.-"The Ozer Method: A Breakthrough Problem Solving Technique
    for Parents." 1982-Morrow - New York, NY
Parrino, John J.-"From Panic to Power-The Positive Use of Stress"
    1979-John Wiley & Sons, New York, NY
Pascale, Richard T. & Anthony Athos-"The Art of Japanese Management"
    1981-Simon & Schuster - New York, NY
Peters, Thomas J. & Robert Waterman, Jr.-"In Search of Excellence"
    1982-Harper & Row - New York, NY
Progoff, Ira-"At A Journal Workshop" - 1975 - Dialogue House
    Library; 80 E. 11th St., New York, NY 10003
Robbins, Anthony-"Unlimited Power." 1986-Simon & Schuster - NY, NY
Rogers, Carl R. & Richard E. Farson - "Active Listening"
    1957-Industrial Relations Center of the University of Chicago
    The University of Chicago, 1225 E. 60th St., Chicago, IL
Ross, Percy & Dick Samson-"Ask for the Moon and Get It!"
    1987-G.P. Putnam's Sons - New York, NY
Rudwick, Bernard H.-"Solving Management Problems: A Systems
    Approach to Planning and Control" 1979-Wiley & Sons, New York
Scheele, Adele M.-"Skills for Success"
    1979-William Morrow & Co. - New York, NY
Schoennauer, Alfred W.W.-"Problem-Finding and Problem-Solving"
    1981-Nelson-Hall - Chicago, IL
Scott, Dru, Ph.D.-"How to Put More Time in Your Life."
    1980 - Rawson, Wade Publishers; 630 3rd Ave., New York, NY 10017
Siegel, Bernard M.D.-"Love, Medicine & Miracles"
    1988-Harper & Row - New York, NY
Smith, Manuel J.,Ph.D.-"When I Say No I Feel Guilty"
    1973 - Dial Press; 1 Dag Hammarskjold Plaza, New York, NY 10017
Souviney, Randall-"Solving Problems Kids Care About"
    Goodyear Publishing Co., Santa Monica, CA
Tarr, Graham-"The Management of Problem-Solving: Positive Results From
    Productive Thinking" 1973-Wiley & Sons - New York, NY
Unamuno y Jugo, Miguel de-"Perplexities and Paradoxes" (Essays)
    Trans. by Stuart Gross - 1945 - N.Y. Philosophical Library

APPENDIX II

AVAILABLE PROBLEM-SOLVING SERVICES

On the cover of this text you were given a money-back guarantee by the author if you met certain conditions and still did not solve the problem you intended to solve when you bought the book. The first condition is that your problem must *not* be of the kind which is specifically treated by licensed professionals, such as doctors, attorneys, psychiatrists, CPAs, securities consultants, family guidance counselors or practitioners of other regulated services. Specifically the guarantee covers solutions for career, personal goal and business problems, provided they do not fall into one of the regulated categories noted above. The guarantee does not mean that *every* problem will definitely be solved by applying these techniques. It merely means the author is willing to refund the price of the book if the book does not help you accomplish what you hoped it would. In lieu of a refund, you may elect to have a one-time correspondence consultation with the author (see below).

The second condition to qualify for a refund is to supply the author with a record in writing of your efforts (1) to work through all of the checklists, (2) to design an effective problem-solving strategy, and (3) to apply all of the steps in your strategy to bring about a resolution of your problem. If you have worked through all of these steps and still not resolved your problem, send in your written report. The author will refund the price of the book in full or, if you choose, will assist you with your problem through a one-time correspondence exchange.

If you wish further assistance on solving problems of the kind addressed by this book, the author offers consulting-by-correspondence for a fee. This means you may write (or tape) a description of your problem and your efforts to solve it and send it to the author at Octagon Press. Your problem will be read and evaluated, and additional coaching or instruction will be provided by mail for an hourly fee. Typewritten requests for help are more quickly and easily processed than hand-written or taped requests, and so the total charge for such assistance is usually less.

The normal fee for a correspondence consultation per hour varies from $25.00 per hour for general personal consultation to $100.00 or more per hour for detailed business analysis and consultation. Personal goal and career-oriented problems can usually be read, evaluated, and supplied with a response in as little as half an hour, at a cost to you of about $12.50 plus postage (at this time). If you include a request for a rate-quotation when you send in your problem, you should receive that quotation in less than a week when postal conditions are normal.

Additional correspondence assistance is provided as an educational service only, and is not guaranteed in any way. You, the student, are fully responsible for successfully learning and applying the additional recommended techniques.

Address correspondence to: Thomas B. Franklin,
OCTAGON PRESS, P.O. Box 36854, Los Angeles, CA 90036

APPENDIX III

ABOUT THE AUTHOR

THOMAS B. FRANKLIN, author, publisher, consultant, lecturer, seminar leader and entrepreneur, has made several major career changes in thirty years of professional life. He began his undergraduate work at Chicago Teacher's College and obtained certification from the Manner's Conservatory of Music in Chicago, Illinois, with a major in Music Education. He taught music at the Conservatory and in his own music school until called into the U.S. Army where he served as Assistant Musical Director for a Second U.S. Army Special Services touring unit.

While in the military, Mr. Franklin learned of new research into processes which could greatly increase human intelligence, reaction time and performance ability. The U.S. Army Research Institute, The National Science Foundation and the U.S. Office of Naval Research have jointly funded an annual symposium held by the International Association for the Study of Attention and Performance since 1966. Prior to that, Mr. Franklin was attracted to a privately conducted experimental program showing I.Q. increases of between 25 and 50 points. As a result of his participation in this program he experienced an I.Q. increase of 30 points and joined Mensa, the high I.Q. society. He also accepted a position as Director of the Personal Efficiency Foundation, first in Washington D.C., and then in New York City, where he administered I.Q. and aptitude tests. In 1968 and 1969 he participated in an advanced developmental program in Sussex, England, which resulted in a Master's Equivalency certificate in Human Development.

During the 1970s and 1980s Mr. Franklin has specialized in computer systems, training programs and private consulting in the Los Angeles area, stressing developmental techniques in career advancement, attention control skills, communication skills and listening and comprehension skills. He is the author of an earlier specialized handbook on attention control development entitled "Attention Control Fundamentals". He is a long standing member of American Mensa, Ltd., the American Society for Training and Development, Toastmasters, International (in which he has held all officer positions including club president), the National Federation of Independent Business (in which he is a member of the Action Council) and the Economic Literacy Council of California (in which he is a member of the Board of Governors). He is currently writing a third book on high-performance development and delivering training and private consulting for his own consulting firm in the southern California area. He resides in Los Angeles with his wife.++

COMPUTER SOFTWARE

THE SOLVER—Interactive Q&A Problem Solving Software
(Scheduled for late 1989 or 1990) 99.95

SEASONAL GIFTS & SPECIALTY ITEMS

Full Year Calendar, with Octagon Chart (11x17) 9.95
The Problem-Solving Power "Thinker" T-Shirt................14.95
The Problem-Solving Power "Thinker" Sweat-Shirt...........24.95
The Problem-Solving Power "Thinker" Bumper Sticker.......4.95

FREE INFORMATION

Listing of luncheon and after-dinner talk topics by the author.
★ *Call for open booking dates for your company, club or organization.*

Quarterly schedule of Workshops & Seminars by the author.
★ *Call for open booking dates for your company, club or organization.*

TO ORDER ADDITIONAL PROBLEM-SOLVING PRODUCTS:

Make a check payable to OCTAGON ENTERPRISES for the amount of your purchase, plus $1.00 shipping and handling charge for every $5.00 of merchandise ordered.
*(When ordering in the State of California, enclose 6.5 % sales tax).

Then mail your order to:

OCTAGON   PRESS
P. O. Box 36854
Los Angeles, CA 90036

(Allow 4 to 6 weeks delivery time)

PROBLEM SOLVING POWER!
ADDITIONAL PROBLEM-SOLVING PRODUCTS

COURSES

Become a problem-solving consultant! Do the PROBLEM-SOLVING
POWER Correspondence Course: 24 lessons 250.00

CHARTS (on heavy stock)

The *SUPER-SOLVER/SUPER-PROBLEM* chart—8.5x11 .....2.95
The *SUPER-SOLVER/SUPER-PROBLEM* chart—11x17 ......4.95
The *SUCCESS/FAILURE SPECTRUM* chart—8.5x11..........2.95
The *SUCCESS/FAILURE SPECTRUM* chart—11x17...........4.95
The *POWER SOLUTION STRATEGY GRID* chart—8.5x11 ..2.95
The *POWER SOLUTION STRATEGY GRID* chart—11x17 ...4.95
The *OCTAGON STRATEGIES* chart—8.5x11.....................2.95
The *OCTAGON STRATEGIES* chart—11x17.....................4.95

BOOKS AND BOOKLETS

The original book: *PROBLEM SOLVING POWER!* 14.95
Your *CHECKLISTS FOR POWER SOLUTIONS—*
Checklists & Guide Sheets..5.95
CHECKLIST BOOK FOR WORKSHOP LEADERS (8.5x11).9.95
T'n'T (Tips'n'Tricks) on Problem-Solving.
From reader's letters and author's responses 2.95
Career Change Problem Solving T'n'T (Tips'n'Tricks).
From reader's letters and author's responses 2.95
Small Business Problem Solving T'n'T (Tips'n'Tricks).
From reader's letters and author's responses 2.95
Women in Business Problem Solving T'n'T (Tips'n'Tricks).
From reader letters and business-woman associate's responses ...2.95
Personal Goal Problem Solving T'n'T (Tips'n'Tricks).
From reader's letters and author's responses 2.95

CASSETTE TAPES

Selected Readings From PROBLEM-SOLVING POWER
By the author (Most chapters available)............................9.95
*CHECKLIST QUESTIONS — Asked With Motivatonal
Emphasis —* By the author 9.95

(Continued overleaf)
O C T A G O N   P R E S S
P.O. Box 36854 — Los Angeles, CA 90036
ISBN 0-925053-01-5